25/5/06

"Ever since *The Inner Game of Tennis*, I've been fascinated and have personally benefited by the incredibly empowering insights flowing out of Gallwey's Self One/Self Two analysis. This latest

o

le

–
e
n
is
it
–
e

s
r
)

s
y
ɔ
n
ɪ,

';
p

THE
INNER GAME
OF
WORK

Absolut: Biography of a Bottle
Carl Hamilton
1-58799-137-3

*eBoys: The True Story of the Six Tall Men Who Backed eBay, Webvan,
and Other Billion-Dollar Start-Ups*
Randall E. Stross
1-58799-135-7

Investing: The Last Liberal Art
Robert G. Hagstrom
1-58799-138-1

*Now or Never: How Companies Must Change Today to Win the Battle
for the Internet Customer*
Mary Modahl
1-58799-041-5

THE
INNER GAME
OF
WORK

Overcoming Mental Obstacles for
Maximum Performance

W. Timothy Gallwey

THOMSON
™
TEXERE

Australia · Canada · Mexico · Singapore · Spain · United Kingdom · United States

THOMSON

TEXERE

**The Inner Game of Work: Overcoming Mental Obstacles
for Maximum Performance**
W. Timothy Gallwey

Published in 2002 by arrangement with Random House, Inc. by TEXERE, part of the Thomson Corporation. TEXERE, Thomson, and Thomson logo are trademarks used herein under license. For more information, contact TEXERE, 300 Park Avenue South, New York, NY 10010 or find us on the Web at www.etexere.com.

A CIP catalogue record for this book is available from the British Library.

ISBN 1-58799-047-4

4 5 6 7 09 08 07 06

Project managed by Macfarlane Production Services, Dunstable, Bedfordshire, England (e-mail: macfarl@aol.com).

Printed and bound in Great Britain by T.J. International Ltd.

To Leslye,
without whose love, care, support, and endurance
this work would not have been completed

Contents

Acknowledgments

With great appreciation to the following people for their generous help in the writing of this book and with special thanks to EF, whose unique insights contributed so substantially to its core ideas.

EF	Bill Wishard	John Horton
Kathleen Lancaster	Chunka Mui	John Kirk
Lee Boudreaux	Chuck Nathan	John von Teuber
Leslye Deitch	Dianne Cory	John Whitmore
Mary Wishard	Erica Anderson	Loring Baker
Owen Plant	Graham Alexander	Mitch Ditkoff
R.J. Rawat	Graham Woolf	Michael Bolger
Sean Brawley	Irene Gallwey	Ole Grunbaum
William Kasoff	Jean Marie Bonthous	Pia Grunbaum
Tim Andrews	Joe Simonet	Prentis Uchida
	Valerio Pascotto	

Preface

by Peter Block

So much is changing in the way we do business, the capacity to adapt and to shift our thinking is critical to success. The challenge is how to transform institutions that have been hardwired for consistency, control, and predictability into cultures where learning, surprise, and discovery are truly valued.

The Inner Game of Work helps us define the landscape of what has become known as a "learning organization." In this book, any manager or employee who has the courage and commitment to really learn about learning will find concepts and practices that can turn the intention of a learning organization into a day-to-day, lived experience.

Most of the traditional strategies for creating a learning organization have involved extracurricular activities. We conduct training events, special programs, and meetings about creating a learning culture. One side effect of these special efforts is that they reinforce the limiting belief that learning and doing are separate and competing activities. We struggle with the tension between how much learning we can afford before it starts interfering with producing. We worry about the "transfer" of learning: how to take the learning and bring it "back" into the workplace. The Inner Game resolves the tension between learning and doing by showing us that they are both part of a bigger whole.

Tim Gallwey's ideas about learning have, from the beginning, been uniquely insightful and radically practical. In 1976, Tim Gallwey's *The Inner Game of Tennis* profoundly changed the way I thought about many things, not just tennis, and twenty-three years later, its influence is still strong. It showed me, for the first time, that our efforts to improve ourselves and our performance actually interfere with what we hope to achieve. Tim challenged much of what we believe about teaching and learning by revealing that much of the teaching we do is actually hostile to learning. *The Inner Game of Work* brings these insights directly into the workplace.

The idea that our standard methods of teaching and coaching reduce performance is radical. Most educational institutions and workplaces rely heavily on instruction and direction, so if all these efforts at improvement are not useful, we had better pay attention. Plus, if instruction doesn't work, what does? Many writers describe what is wrong with the world, but they become theoretical or abstract when it comes time for real workable alternatives.

What is special about Tim's work is that he not only defines the nature of our interference, he offers beautifully concrete ways to increase learning and performing that minimize instruction and direction. This is his genius. He understands how we learn and has spent his life creating ways we can un-manage ourselves toward higher achievement. The Inner Game has changed the way many people relate to their work, and perhaps even more important, it offers institutions a way to simultaneously create learning, improve performance, and foster a more satisfying workplace.

Becoming a learning culture is very demanding. It requires more than most of us realize and asks managers to have a deep enough commitment to learning and performance to give up some control. The challenge of the Inner Game is that it requires faith and a great deal of unlearning of bad habits. The Inner Game demands that we value awareness, consciousness, and paying attention to what is happening within and around us. No easy assignment. In our Western culture, as soon as you say the words *awareness* and *attention,* it is labeled New Age and the theory is dismissed as a form of California dreaming. It's not.

The fundamental question is, What is possible in the workplace? Can we have good performance, high enjoyment, and high learning all at the same time? This raises the deeper question of what is the purpose of work. Is the purpose of work to deliver institutional outcomes—greater profit, higher service levels, market domination? The economists, the financial community, and the business press have a simple answer to this question: show me the money.

For most people, though, the question of purpose is more complex. They accept the need for economic success, but there is more to work than meets the wallet. People care about the workplace culture, its relationships, the opportunity to fulfill their potential, and the chance to learn and improve their skills. We often treat this as a tension between management and employees, but that is not the real issue. It is an individual, internal struggle. We are constantly torn between getting results and living a process that is humanly satisfying.

It is in this arena that the Inner Game offers hope. Tim constantly raises the question of what game we are playing. Can we play a satisfying Inner Game and at the same time meet the requirements of the outer game?

Finding some cohesion between inner and outer, however, demands some radical experimentation. We need to try new structures, new practices, and new ways to honor the complexity of the question.

Many years ago, Tim and I attended a national sales conference for a large American corporation. It goes without saying that salespeople like to compete. They not only like to compete, they believe in it. Competition is the point of it all; to be a winner in the marketplace is both the goal and the reward. That is true for both the business and the person. This whole sales conference was, in fact, an assembly of winners, an affirmation that they were the best in the company and probably the best in the industry, perhaps in the world.

Following a presentation on Inner Game coaching, Tim

agreed to manage the annual tennis tournament, a tradition at every sales conference. After all, winners love a tournament, and here they had a well-known author/tennis coach available to be maître d' of the event. Tim, though, was not satisfied in simply presiding. He thought that the tennis tournament could provide a unique learning experience for each participant by asking the question, What game are you really playing?

Tim suggested that the winners of each match would be out of the tournament, and the player who lost would advance to the next round. Think of this: the loser was rewarded for losing, and the winner was sent to the sidelines. If this is the structure, what is the point of playing if "winning" got you nowhere? Well, this *was* the point. Each player had to confront the question of why he was playing the game. The conventional answer, especially among salespeople, is that they play to win. Tim's answer was that there is a better game to play, and that is to play to learn, to play to fulfill your own potential. And ironically, if you do this, you will actually get better performance.

The intent of a tournament where losers advanced and winners went home was that it would be unclear to the players whether it was in their interest to win or lose. If they beat their opponent, they would, in effect, be a loser. If they lost to their opponent, they would be treated as a winner. In the face of this, they were free to shift their focus from winning or losing to simply playing for the experience itself, playing to see how good a player they could become. Philosophically, they were asked to stop dancing to the tune defined by the external world around them and encouraged to play according to their own internal message center. The tennis tournament offers a metaphor for what is possible in the workplace. No matter what structure we are given, there is always the possibility of transforming the dominant cultural habit into an unpredictable event where learning is more likely to happen.

Now, I am not suggesting that all tournaments reward those who lose, but this kind of thoughtful and selective experimentation is what separates organizations that simply survive from those that excel. This willingness to question the conventional wisdom makes the difference. And, in fact, many management practices that would have seemed radical fifteen years ago are now accepted in countless corporations. For example,

- Teams are now self-organizing and do most of the tasks that bosses used to do.
- Workers inspect their own work, where previously it had always been thought that third-party inspection was essential to good quality.
- Bosses are now evaluated by their subordinates.
- Suppliers are now treated as part of the producing organization and included in planning and decisions.
- Salespeople can make customer-service decisions that used to be centralized and required two levels of approval.

Each of these, and many more, questions what was once held sacred as the prerogative of management and essential to maintaining adequate controls. The tennis tournament still stands out vividly in my mind as an early indicator of the kind of experimentation that a real learning environment will require. It questioned its own deeper purpose, it varied enough from tradition that it left all involved a little uncomfortable, and it ultimately became a source of energy and play that brought some life to the whole sales event.

The role of coaches and the constant re-forming of our understanding of purpose and structures seem essential to the thinking about the role management can play in creating an environment where learning is valued. What is required is the belief that learning and performing are one and the same. High performers are people who simply learn faster. We learn faster when we pay attention and see the world for what it truly is, not for what it should have been. Learning then becomes a function of awareness more than instruction; it is seeing clearly what is happening around you, seeing it without much judgment and without an instinct to control and shape all that you touch.

Learning is retarded in conditions of high anxiety and low acceptance. For most tasks, people have the intellectual knowledge to perform well; they just have a hard time acting on what they know. And this is one profound insight of the Inner Game. We do not need to learn more from a boss or expert: we need to change the way we apply what already exists within us. Increasing pressure for results is more paralyzing than liberating, even though this idea goes against the conventional wisdom of the culture.

These ideas have widespread implications for the next generation of workplace changes. If we really want best performance, we would redesign common practices that try to improve performance through instruction and traditional management intervention. For example, we would stop rank ordering individuals and units as a motivational/reward device. We would change the rhetoric from being about winning and make it about learning. Performance appraisals would stop being evolutions of an employee's strengths and weaknesses and become a dialogue between a manager and an employee about what each is experiencing and what that means. We would treat employees as autonomous, self-developing agents. It means our educational efforts would shift from a focus on training to a focus on learning, and these would be designed around the learner's experience rather than the teacher's expertise. We would question the value of modeling tapes, training with predefined, predictable behaviors as an outcome.

In every workplace we need to win. The workplace is not a social event, and our survival is always on the line. This doesn't answer the fundamental questions of purpose and meaning, both for the institution and the individual. In a quiet and concrete way, the Inner Game argues for creating institutions that can offer people deeper meaning than just profitability, while at the same time achieving economic success. How can we play a game where the human spirit is validated and still get good work done? Most organizations have this desire, but they are still wedded to a way of thinking that treats the person as a means to an economic end. The business has to prosper, but the person needs to find purpose beyond that and needs to do so in a way that nurtures rather than burns. Placing a higher value on learning, and the awareness that learning demands, offers us hope that this is possible.

The Inner Game of Work is a product of Tim's twenty-plus years in the field, of his bringing Inner Game ideas into the business world. It requires the reader to suspend judgment and be open to the possibility that there are fundamentally new ways to realize our intentions and desires.

Enjoy this book. Take it seriously. Put it to work, and over time, what was stressful will become merely interesting, what you avoided will become attractive, and what seemed futile will become a source of possibility.

PETER BLOCK is the best-selling author of *Flawless Consulting: A Guide to Getting Your Expertise Used; The Empowered Manager: Positive Political Skills at Work;* and *Stewardship: Choosing Service over Self-Interest.*

Introduction

The Quest to Work Free

Man was born free, but everywhere he's in chains.

— Jean-Jacques Rousseau,
eighteenth-century philosopher

I have embarked on a quest to work free. I am not interested in a conceptual ideal of freedom at work, but in something more practical. I want to honor that part of myself that is inherently free regardless of its circumstances. My quest is to acknowledge this self and to allow it to be expressed at work.

It has been in the field of work, more than in any other human endeavor, that freedom has been most seriously compromised. Have we not all felt the chains that bind us at work? The chains of "must," "have to," "do it or else"—the chains of fear and external pressures. The prevailing definition of work has come to mean something that I'd rather not be doing if I had the choice.

Each time I take a committed step toward working free, I can feel the chains begin to tighten. The bonds of unconscious habit pull me back as if I'm attached by a rubber band to a post. The first few steps are not so hard, but tension builds as I take each step away from my routines. When stretched to the limit, I have felt the force snap me all the way back in the opposite direction, leaving me no choice but to start the journey again. Perhaps the quest for true freedom must at some point expose that central post to which the band is tied. This freedom I pursue is an innate freedom, not one granted by a person or society. Its pursuit requires a fundamental redefinition of "work."

My quest to work free began in the early seventies when I left a relatively secure career in higher education to think about what I wanted to do with my life. Then, with little intention besides earning some interim income, I began teaching tennis, and soon found myself in the midst of fundamental discoveries about learning and coaching that subsequently became the subject of *The Inner Game of Tennis*. The simple principles and methods of the Inner Game were based on a profound trust in the student's natural capability to learn from direct experience.

These Inner Game principles have stood the test of time and have been applied successfully to countless fields over the past two decades. The Inner Game is a viable alternative to traditional command-and-control methodologies that are taken for granted at work as well as at play. It provides a promising start on the journey toward working free. Success on this path will depend primarily on the readers' willingness to grant a radical level of trust to *themselves*.

THE
INNER GAME
OF
WORK

1

A BETTER WAY TO CHANGE

The essence of all that I've learned through my exploration of the Inner Game can be boiled down to one sentence: I have found a better way to change. Though I discovered it while teaching tennis players how to make changes in their forehands, backhands, and serves, the principles and methods that worked for developing skills on the tennis court apply to making improvements in any activity. This book is about how to make changes in the way we work. It is about how to make work *work* for us.

We are constantly told that we live in an age of change, and nowhere are we told more frequently that we *have to change* than in the workplace. The change may be a massive corporate reorganization of which you are a small part, or a midsize change "in the way we do things in this department," or perhaps just an individual change required by your manager after your latest performance review. Even when the impetus for change does not come from outside, most of us want to make changes in how we work and in the results we are getting. When you go to a bookstore you find that the largest category is self-improvement, books that tell you how to make a change in *yourself.* We talk about everything that needs to change, but how well do we understand how to go about *making* a change?

My first career was as an educator, a profession still notorious for being slow to embrace real change. Ironically, education is supposed to be about learning, and thus about change. It should provide insight and wisdom about change as well as set a good example. Yet it was not until I left the corridors of institutionalized education that I began to discover a profoundly different approach to learning and change.

Origins of the Inner Game

My insights into the Inner Game started with the playing and teaching of sports in the early 1970s. In hindsight, I can see why sports made such a good laboratory for exploring learning and change. It is because performance in sports is so directly observable, and the goals are so clear, that differences in performance are more visible. My initial laboratories were tennis, skiing, and golf, sports in which one is made all too aware of the great disparity between one's best and worst performance. This disparity cannot be attributed to lack of talent alone. It points directly to the way in which we go about learning or making changes in performance.

Two observations stand out as I reflect on my early experience with coaching performance in sports. The first is that almost everyone who came to me for a lesson was *trying very hard* to fix some aspect of their game that they didn't like. They expected *me* to provide the remedy for their problem. The second is the relative effortlessness with which change for the better took place when they *stopped* trying so hard and trusted in their capacity to learn from their own experience. There was a stark contrast between the forced mode of learning and the natural learning seen in the early development of all young children.

Observing the normal interaction between a student and his tennis teacher provides a window into the way we have all learned to make changes. Normally the player approaches the teacher with some kind of complaint, either about one of his strokes or about his results. "I'm not getting enough power on my serve," he might say, or "I need to make a change in my backhand." The teacher watches the student demonstrate his current stroke, then he compares what he sees to a model in his head of "the correct stroke." This model is based on what the teacher has been taught is the "right way." Looking through the lens of this model, the coach sees all the differences between "what is" and "what should be," and begins the hard work of getting the two to match.

To accomplish this task, the teacher may use a great variety of instructions, but there is a single common context. Perhaps he says, "You should step into the ball as you make contact, with your weight on your front foot. You shouldn't take your racket back so high on your backswing. Your follow-through should be done more like this." The common context is: "I will tell you what you should and shouldn't do."

Faced with this series of should and shouldn't commands, the student's pattern of behavior becomes quite predictable. Placing his trust in the judgmental feedback of the teacher, the student's responsibility becomes merely to do what he's told. Thus he *tries hard* not to do what he shouldn't do and to make himself do what he should. Told that the racket is being taken back too late, the student forces his arm to move back faster. For the student it may *feel* overly tight and awkward, but the teacher sees the response to his command and says "good." What is really being said is "Good, you are trying to obey me." The student comes to associate "good" with this forced and unnatural way of *fixing* his strokes. The teacher provides the "shoulds" and "shouldn'ts," and the student supplies the "trying hard," which is followed by another "good" or "bad" judgment by the coach.

So it goes, over and over again. Change is viewed as a movement from bad to good, defined and initiated by someone other than the one who is making the change. It is done in a judgmental context that usually brings with it resistance, doubt, and fear of failure on the part of the student. Neither student nor teacher is likely to be aware that this approach to change undermines the student's innate eagerness and responsibility for learning. They may struggle with the inherent contradictions in this approach, but it is usually the only way they know.

The Discovery of Self 1 and Self 2

My first insight into another way came the day I stopped trying to *change* the student's swing. Instead I asked myself, "How is learning really taking place?" and "What's going on inside the head of the player when he hits the ball?" It occurred to me that there was a dialogue going on in the player's head, an internal conversation not unlike his external conversation with me. In a commanding tone, the voice in his head would issue teacherlike commands to his body: "Get your racket back early. Step into the ball. Follow through at the shoulders." After the shot, the same voice would deliver its evaluation of the performance and the performer: "That was a terrible shot! You have the worst backhand I've ever seen!"

Is all this inner dialogue really necessary? I wondered. Is it helping the learning process or is it getting in the way? I knew that when great athletes were asked what they were thinking during their best performance, they universally declared that they weren't thinking very much at all. They reported that their minds were quiet and focused. If they thought about their performance at all, it was before or after the activity itself. This was also true in my own experience as a tennis player. When I was playing at my best, I wasn't trying to control my shots with self-instruction and evaluation. It was a much simpler process than that. I saw the ball clearly, chose where I wanted to hit it, and I *let* it happen. Surprisingly, the shots were more controlled when I didn't try to control them.

I gradually realized that my well-intentioned instructions were being internalized by my students as methods of control that were compromising their natural abilities. This critical inner dialogue certainly produced a state of mind very different from the quiet focus reported by the best athletes.

My next question was, "In this inner dialogue, who is talking to whom?" I called the voice giving the commands and making the judgments "Self 1." The one it was talking to, I called "Self 2." What was their relationship? Self 1 was the know-it-all who basically didn't trust Self 2, the one who had to hit the ball. Out of mistrust, Self 1 was trying to control Self 2's behavior using the tactics it had learned from its teachers in the outside world. In other words, the mistrust implied by the judgmental context was being internalized by the student's Self 1. The resulting self-doubt and overcontrol interfered with the natural learning process.

But who is Self 2? Is it that unworthy of trust? In my definition, Self 2 is the human being itself. It embodies all the inherent potential we were born with, including all capacities actualized and not yet actualized. It also embodies our innate ability to learn and to grow any of those inherent capacities. It is the self we all enjoyed as young children.

All the evidence pointed to the fact that our best performance happened when Self 1's voice was quiet and Self 2 was allowed to hit the ball undisturbed. While Self 1 might be commanding the body with the vague instruction "Get the racket back early," Self 2 was doing something far more precise. Calculating the eventual position of the parabolic arc of the ball, it was issuing hundreds of exact nonverbal instructions to scores of muscle groups that allowed the body to hit the ball and send it to the desired location on the other side of the net, all the while taking into account the speed of the ball, the wind, and the last-second movement of the opponent. Which self was more trustworthy?

It was like a dime-store computer giving orders to a billion-dollar mainframe, then wanting to take the credit for the best outcomes while blaming the mainframe for the worst. It is humbling to realize that the voice giving the controlling demands and criticisms was not really as intelligent as the one receiving them! The invented Self 1 was not as smart as the natural self. In short, the cartoon character Pogo was right when he proclaimed, "I have met the enemy, and it is us."

This Self 1 dialogue doesn't just plague beginners in their learning process. It occurs at all levels of performance. Even professionals who have enjoyed performing at the very top levels in their field are vulnerable to crises in confidence. As I was writing this chapter, I heard from two professional athletes who said they were "losing their inner game." One was a golfer who had been on the PGA tour for eight years, who complained that he couldn't silence the critical voice in his head after hitting one or two bad shots in a round. "I'm letting the pressure get to me. I'm getting down on myself when I'm not performing well, and my self-confidence is suffering." The other was a basketball player with more than ten years in the NBA who played on some of the best teams in the world. He said that *The Inner Game of Tennis* had been like a bible to him for most of the past decade and had significantly enhanced his performance on the court. But recently he began losing confidence in his shooting, the strongest part of his game. He complained, "I'm talking to myself constantly on the court, and I hate it. I miss the euphoria that comes from being totally immersed in the game without so many thoughts in my head."

I felt a great respect for the courage it took for these professional athletes to admit to themselves that their problem was not just technical. They realized they were getting in their own way, and they reached out for coaching.

The Cycle of Self-Interference

Perhaps we all realize that as human beings we have a tendency to get in our own way, but I want to take a closer look at how it actually happens. Take the simple action of hitting a single tennis ball. The player *sees* an image of an approaching ball, then *responds* by moving into position and striking the ball, producing the *results* of the action. Perception, response, results. The basic elements of any human action are summarized in this simple sequence of events.

But usually it's not quite so simple. Between the perception and the action, there is some *interpretation*. After the results and before the next action, there is yet more thinking. At each stage, *meaning* is being attributed to each part of the action and often to the performer himself. These meanings can have a huge impact on the player's performance.

Take a player whose Self 1 has convinced him that he has a weak backhand. As he sees the ball coming toward his backhand, he thinks, "Uh-oh, here comes a difficult shot." The thought flashes across his mind faster than the tennis ball can move a foot. What is merely a yellow ball traveling at a certain speed and trajectory is now perceived as a *threat* flying through the air. A shot of adrenaline surges through his body. His racket is jerked back defensively as his feet shuffle backward, to delay the inevitable error he thinks is about to occur. At the last possible moment, the racket slashes down angrily but ineffectually toward the ball, which floats high above the net for an easy put-away by the opponent. Self 1 is there, ready with the self-condemning comment, "That was a terrible shot! I've got the worst backhand on the planet!" Now with his confidence further undermined, the next ball is perceived as an even greater threat. The cycle of interference is set to repeat itself.

Self 1 introduces distortion into every element of the action. The distortion in self-image prompts a distortion in perception that leads to a distorted response that confirms the originally distorted self-image.

Finding a Better Way to Make a Change

How do you break the cycle of Self 1 interference? A significant breakthrough in answering this question came when I realized

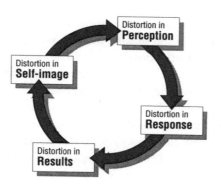

that the traditional method of learning focused on behavior—the player's response—without ever dealing with the root problem—the player's distortion in perception.

After all, it was the *perception* of the ball as a threat that had created multiple faults in the behavior. What would happen to those behaviors if, through coaching, the ball ceased to be a threat and simply became a ball again? Furthermore, what would happen if the player's judgment of himself and his performance could be replaced by a nonjudgmental observation of fact?

As I explored answers to these questions, a different and more elegant approach to learning and coaching emerged. It was based on principles that could be summarized in three words: *awareness, trust,* and *choice.* Elaborated slightly, the principles were (1) nonjudgmental awareness is curative; (2) trust Self 2 (my own and the student's); and (3) leave primary learning choices with the student.

1 The Power of Nonjudgmental Awareness—Once I realized that my "should and shouldn't" instructions were part of what was getting in the way, I began to explore ways of helping the student learn without them. My initial goal became simply to help the student increase awareness of the flight of the oncoming ball.

When my student complained about his faulty backhand, I would tell him that I wanted to postpone *fixing* it until later. All I wanted him to do now was to observe some detail of the ball. For example, I might ask the student to notice whether the ball was falling, rising, or level at the moment of contact with the racket. I would hasten to say that I wasn't asking him to make any change, but just to observe what was happening. As the student became absorbed in watching the flight of the ball, he would become "distracted" from his Self 1 efforts to control the stroke, and for the moment, all perceived threat would disappear.

"That ball was still rising when it hit the racket. That one was level. And that one was coming down from its highest point." When I could hear the neutrality of observation in his tone of voice, I knew that his mind-set was no longer a judgmental one, at least for the moment. What amazed me at first, but which I later came to expect, was that in this nonjudgmental mode of observation of the ball, many of the technical elements of his swing would change spontaneously! For example, his feet would no longer retreat, the racket would not be jerked back so harshly, and the front foot would naturally move to a position to support his forward momentum. In a matter of a few moments, his swing would look substantially improved. Yet there had been no technical instructions, and in many cases the player didn't even know the changes had taken place.

Why did these positive changes occur? Was it as simple as getting Self 1 out of the way and allowing Self 2 to learn how to hit the shot? One answer is that when the initial *perception* of the ball as a threat was removed, the elements of defensive behavior (backward movement and slashing at the ball) vanished also. Instead, the body was allowed its natural response to the perception of the ball, which was to step into it and hit it. Sensing that the coach was not interested in judging his stroke, but simply in his observation of the ball, the student's mind was, for the moment, relatively free of self-judgment and Self 1–type controls. As a result, his movements would be smoother and more precise. The smooth swing coupled with the clearer perception of the ball made for better contact with the ball. This *felt* better and naturally produced better results. As the student observed his improved performance, natural self-confidence grew in place of self-doubt. The cycle of self-interference had been reversed.

As long as focus was maintained on some neutral but critical variable (for example, the speed, position, or height of the ball), I could count on seeing steady and relatively effortless improvement in strokes, without a single technical instruction. At first, it seemed like magic. Then I realized it was natural magic—the way learning was supposed to be. As coach, my first responsibility was to maintain a nonjudgmental focus, provide appropriate opportunity for natural learning, and stay out of the way. Secondarily, my job was to help the student maintain focus while trusting in Self 2's capacity to learn directly from experience.

The same principle of nonjudgmental awareness worked

when the focus was shifted from the ball to the player's actions. For example, when I asked the student to pay attention to his movements—but without making any effort to change them—change would begin to take place spontaneously.

This is not to say that errors ceased to occur. But in the context of nonjudgmental awareness, the response of both coach and player to errors was different. And as soon as either student or coach broke the context of nonjudgmental awareness, by making negative or positive evaluations of a shot, the perception of threat would usually return and trigger the cycle of self-interference.

Thus the first step in this better way to change lies in a non-judgmental acknowledgment of things as they *are*. Paradoxically, it is conscious acceptance of oneself and one's actions *as they are* that frees up both the incentive and the capacity for spontaneous change.

2. Trust in Self 2—Perhaps the most difficult thing about this new learning process was that both the coach and the student had to learn to trust the *natural* learning process. For me as coach, this meant I had to stop my conditioned response to make a corrective comment each time I saw a fault in the student's swing. For the student it meant not depending on technical instructions to improve his strokes. We had to trust that as our awareness increased, effective learning and change would take place. The coach's actions could either support the student's self-trust or undermine it. Time and again when I was patient enough to let go of my desire to control the learning, it would take place at its own pace and in a much more elegant and effective way than ever could have happened using a teacher-centered command-and-control methodology.

It was hard to argue with the results. After seeing hundreds of examples of players at all levels improving without technical instructions, I have found this trust easier and easier to come by. The more I trusted this natural process as the coach, the easier it was for students to trust themselves and their own capacity to learn from experience.

As the student sees continuing improvement take place without the "should and shouldn't" instructions, his self-trust grows stronger. Soon he realizes that learning in this way is a very different experience from that of being fit into a preconceived model of correct form. It is the experience of learning from the inside out, instead of from the outside in, and it is always a beautiful thing to see. Exercising trust in Self 2 seems like you are losing control, but the fact is that you are gaining control by letting go of an inferior means of control. This is a lesson that both coach and performer have to learn over and over in each new situation.

To realize that the final authority and responsibility for learning lies within the individual doing the learning is contrary to much of our conditioning. Yet this principle of trust in oneself is at the heart of finding a better way to change.

3. Keep Choice with the Choice-maker—The third principle of the Inner Game approach to change is about choice and commitment. Awareness and trust cannot work unless there is a desired outcome. The student can watch the ball, but if he doesn't want to hit it over the net and into the court, the development of tennis skills won't happen. Clarity of desired outcome is essential for the principle of awareness to work. The question then becomes, who is choosing the outcome?

In my old teacher-centered approach, I wanted to retain most of the important choices made in the tennis lesson. Once the student made the choice to take a lesson, I was in charge. I would want to make the choice about what stroke needed work, which elements of that stroke I would start with, and the best remedy to apply. It was very much like the traditional doctor-patient relationship: "I'm the expert. I'll diagnose what is wrong and prescribe the cure. Your job is to do what I tell you, and have faith that if you do, you will get better."

I had to learn to give the choices back to the student. Why? Because the learning takes place within the student. The student makes the choices that ultimately control whether learning takes place or doesn't. In the end, I realized that the student was responsible for the learning choices and I was responsible for the quality of the external learning environment.

What this meant was that I would ask the student what he wanted to improve and why. I saw my role as coach to understand where the student wanted to go and to help him get there. The student might start the coaching conversation by saying "I want to improve my backhand" and end up with a goal of "I want to be able to hit ten out of ten topspin backhand passing shots down the line off the serve."

My role was not just to make the immediate goal as clear as possible but to evoke from the student the underlying purpose and motivation for reaching the goal. Allowing the student to be more aware of the choices he was making and the reasons behind those choices was an essential part of this learning process. The student felt more in control and as a natural consequence was willing to accept more responsibility, and exercise greater initiative and creativity in achieving their goal. Equally important, it greatly diminished the resistance to change that was inherent in the old command-and-control model. There's an old saying, "When you insist, I resist." It is natural for the human being to resist encroachment on his boundaries, and when the resistance isn't expressed directly, it will come out indirectly. Either way, the resistance is detrimental to the desired outcome.

To students who were used to the command-and-control model, being granted a greater degree of choice was often disconcerting. But as each student learned that his choices were not going to be judged by the coach as right or wrong, he accepted his role as the choice-maker and he accepted responsibility for the outcome of those choices.

Many positive elements for learning and change resulted from this shift. It kept the initiative for learning and change in the hands of the student and gave him or her a greater sense of personal involvement and participation. It prevented the learning from being merely by rote and thus easily forgotten. It allowed for much greater personal involvement on the part of the learner and for changes to take place naturally as true understanding grew. Such learning engages the attitudes and feelings of students and often provokes changes that pervade every aspect of their lives. In short, when the choices for learning and change were allowed to be self-initiated and self-regulated, they became more comprehensive as well as more enjoyable.

Experience with the three principles—awareness, choice, and trust—showed that they were inextricably connected. They were three parts of a whole. *Awareness* was about knowing the present situation with clarity. *Choice* was about moving in a desired direction in the future. And *Trust* in one's own inner resources was the essential link that enabled that movement. Each side of this triangle complemented and supported the other. The more I trusted, the easier it was to be aware. The more aware I was, the easier it was to see my choices. As my understanding of each principle deepened, I saw that they were all I needed to form the basis of a new approach to learning and making changes.

Change could be enjoyable. No one needed to feel manipulated or judged. Experience itself could be the final authority. Change and improvement, without Self 1's interferences, could happen at an accelerated rate and be both reliable and continuous.

I began to believe that *learning to learn* in this way could fundamentally alter the way we go about making changes in ourselves and others.

AWARENESS

CHOICE   TRUST

Myriad Unexpected Applications

When I wrote about my discoveries in *The Inner Game of Tennis,* I had no idea that it would become a best-seller and be read by so many who were not tennis players. I had been told by my publisher that I shouldn't expect a sports book to sell more than about twenty thousand copies. What surprised us both was that hundreds of thousands of non-tennis-players bought the book and applied its methods to improving their personal performance in a wide range of activities. I was amazed by the ingenuity and creativity with which Inner Game principles were applied to vastly different areas, including:

- Attaining peak performance in selling
- Managing corporate change initiatives
- Developing the coaching skills of managers
- Creating "Total Quality Management" programs
- Heightening innovation and creativity
- Parenting
- Improvement in sports of all kinds
- Performing surgery
- Acting, writing, painting, playing and composing music, public speaking
- Teaching, consulting, coaching, counseling
- Reducing stress
- Improving relationships
- Dieting
- Overcoming tobacco, drug, and alcohol addictions
- Advanced structural engineering
- Human–computer interface design

The common denominator here is that these are all activities in which focus of attention and reduction of self-interference made a difference.

From Sports to Work

As the focus of my own career shifted from sports to the field of corporate work, I realized companies had much to gain by learning to access the great reservoir of Self 2 talent in their workforces. Success in this effort would depend on their ability to recognize and reduce the many ways in which their culturally accepted practices contributed to Self 1's interference with that talent.

From the individual worker's point of view, there isn't time to wait for cultural change to take place. Only by starting the process of reducing Self 1 interference within themselves, and perhaps in their work groups, could they hope to access and develop more of their Self 2's latent capabilities.

This understanding could be put into a simple formula that defined the Inner Game.

$$P = p - i$$

Performance = potential − interference

Performance (**P**) in any activity, from hitting a ball to solving a complex business problem, was equal to one's potential (**p**) *after* the interference factor (**i**) had been subtracted from the equation. Performance rarely equals potential. A little self-doubt, an erroneous assumption, the fear of failure, was all it took to greatly diminish one's actual performance.

The Inner Game and the Outer Game

The goal of the Inner Game was to reduce whatever interfered with the discovery and expression of one's full potential. The goal of the outer game was to overcome external obstacles to reach an external goal. Clearly the two games are related. The greater the external challenges accepted by an individual, team, or company, the *more* important it is that there be a minimum of interference occurring from within.

No matter what culture you work in, what kind of work you do, or what your present level of competence is, both inner and outer games are always going on. Progress will always be dependent on both. They are like the two legs of a person: Walking through life is easier if they are approximately the same length. Yet as a culture, we have put much more emphasis on mastering the outer game and making changes in the external world. With science, technology, and the modern information explosion, we have developed a relatively long outer-game leg. But our understanding and control of the Inner Game has not evolved equally.

In this century, if we do not learn some of the basic skills of the Inner Game, our technical progress in the outer game will be of little benefit to mankind. We have a profound need to better understand, and learn to make changes in, the domain we call *ourselves*. And that can happen only if we change in ways that are in harmony with our true nature and not at war with it.

2

THE INNER GAME MEETS CORPORATE AMERICA

One day not long after the publication of *The Inner Game of Tennis,* Archie McGill, then the VP of business marketing at AT&T, unexpectedly showed up in Los Angeles asking for an Inner Game tennis lesson. Pleased and somewhat surprised with both the process and the results, he invited me to lunch to discuss his challenge to change the corporate culture at AT&T. He took about two minutes to describe the complex set of changes that had been set in motion by the Supreme Court's decision that AT&T would have to break up its monopoly in telecommunications.

"If we can't succeed in making this monumental transition from a monopolistic utility to a competitive, market-driven communications enterprise, we will be eaten alive in the new environment. And we have to do it now. We have no choice." His summary was compelling, but his situation seemed light-years away from my experience using Inner Game methods to help students bring out their potential on the tennis courts. So I was quite shocked when McGill asked me for my analysis of the situation.

"So, tell me," he said, in a no-nonsense tone, "what's the *real* problem?" I said nothing for what seemed like a long time. Then a response came from my mouth that surprised me as much for its authority as for its content. "The problem is your people don't know *who* they are," I said emphatically. "Thus, they tend to identify themselves with their roles, their reputations, the company itself, and the current way of doing things. When the stability of any of these factors is threatened, their automatic response is to resist, and to resist as if they were protecting their own selves. Because they are protecting who they think they *are,* they do so with considerable force."

McGill seemed to be paying very close attention and nodded as I spoke. I sensed that I was saying what he had already known to be true at some profound level but had never consciously acknowledged. Quickly I brought the focus of the conversation back to my coaching experience. "What I observed on the tennis courts is that the biggest difficulty in changing a habit is the fact that people have identified themselves with *their* particular way of hitting the ball. It is as if they are saying, 'For better or for worse, this is the way I do it. And don't you dare try to change *me,* even if I ask you to. Furthermore, if you tell me I am doing it wrong, I will take it personally—as if you are saying *You are wrong.* And I don't like that at all, but I won't say so because you are the coach and I'm supposed to at least pretend that I am willing to do it *your* way. But underneath my seeming compliance, I will look for subtle ways of resisting.' Most of us have had to learn creative ways to protect what we think is our personal integrity in the face of efforts from parents, teachers, bosses, to get us to put their agendas before our own. This conflict goes on for most of our lives and we are well versed in the art of resistance."

"You mean, people take the whole thing too personally," Archie said in his own succinct manner. The discussion continued with my experience of how nonjudgmental awareness, respecting choice, and trust could be used as powerful medicines for reducing this age-old conflict and for creating a much better environment for change.

Two days later McGill and four of his top staff were sitting in my living room in California asking me questions about issues of organizational change in which I had little direct experience. Precisely because I knew so little about how organizations worked, I had to draw on my educational and coaching experiences and on what I had learned about how individuals worked. The conversation focused on overcoming the inner obstacles standing in the way of needed change. At the end of three hours of talking about the Inner Game approach—mainly about practical applications of Inner Game methods to changing behavior and attitudes—McGill turned to his staff and asked them three questions:

1. "Is all of this Inner Game stuff relevant to our change process at AT&T?"

Each person in turn agreed that, yes, it was very relevant.

2. "How does the Inner Game process of change compare to the way we are going about changing now?"

Each person gave the same response. "Well, it's pretty much the opposite."

3. "If we wanted to, how would we go about infusing this approach into our change process?"

There was a long pause, then again each gave the same reply: "I don't know."

The meeting closed with McGill assigning an executive named Bill the task of coming up with a plan for the implementation of Inner Game methods in two weeks. Expecting that Bill would want to call me for my input, I waited. Then at the end of two weeks I called him to ask how his task was progressing. He was glad to hear from me but sounded like a man drowning in an ocean of crises. Saying he had not yet produced a plan and was stuck on how to even get started, he asked if I had any advice. Disclaiming any expertise in corporate matters, I said the obvious, "Well, you might try starting with yourselves."

The silence on the phone suggested that Bill was somewhat stunned. "That's the first thing that occurred to me, but I really don't think I could suggest that. McGill would take it as an insult."

"Tell him it was *my* recommendation," I offered.

Though McGill and his direct reports avoided the suggestion of a training directed toward themselves, Archie became a corporate advocate of the Inner Game. Driving to work with SELF 2 on his New Jersey license plate, he began to make a conscious effort to change his own overbearing style of management. He initiated a project to bring Inner Game principles into the core curriculum for the training of all account executives and talked to fellow senior managers in various divisions of the company. Soon my reputation began to grow, and I was invited to contribute to various change initiatives in different parts of the company. These ranged from regular presentations to senior executives at the corporate policy seminars to designing accelerated learning programs for service technicians, and one program that will be discussed in some depth later on, "The Inner Game of Operating."

I was beginning to see how things got done in AT&T's corporate culture and what kept them from getting done. I was impressed and apprehensive at the same time. Many millions of dollars and the jobs of thousands of employees were at stake in the decisions McGill was making. And my advice was being used to inform those decisions. I remember feeling like the character Chauncey Gardiner, played by Peter Sellers, in the movie *Being There*. Being a simple gardener who had no experience in the world outside his garden, he was drawn into a situation where he was asked questions about complex matters by leading economists and government ministers. Chauncey, thinking that they must only be asking him about his garden, would respond with comments about his knowledge of growing roses. The ministers, believing him to be a genius, were taking Chauncey's remarks as metaphors about the state of the economy, and ascribing great wisdom to him while in fact projecting their own meanings to what they were hearing.

Like Chauncey, I understood less than five percent of the highly complex problems facing AT&T. And like Chauncey, I would answer questions in terms of what I knew—overcoming resistance to change and growing human capability. I would find myself in boardrooms at the top floor of AT&T headquarters in Basking Ridge, New Jersey, surrounded by executives, most of whom seemed to have shining bald heads and solemn demeanors, who took copious notes about my explanations of the process of coaching people to play better tennis. Thinking that I knew much more about business than I did, the executives were simply recording reflections of their own profound understanding. The only difference between me and Chauncey was that I *knew* that I didn't know anything about business at their level. But I also knew that my experiences overcoming the obstacles to change and skill development in tennis players were very relevant to the problems of rapid change and training facing these corporate executives.

As a result, I started learning a great deal more about corporate cultures and about what facilitated and what hindered change. My first three observations about corporate change have proven, unfortunately, enduring ones:

1. People in a position to make changes tend to absolve themselves from the need to make the changes in themselves first. Change is something "we" do to "them." Learning is something "they" need to do.

Not surprisingly, the validity of this rule tended to increase as one went up the corporate hierarchy. I found the professional businessman's ego more resistant to change than the professional athlete's. The best athletes seek continuous improvement in their own performance and seek out and welcome help from coaches. But in the corporate hierarchies, even if time could be found to coach others, it was rare to find people who sought coaching for themselves. Ironically, the avoidance of personal engagement in the change process tended to be greater the closer you got to the people responsible for initiating the change in others. It was as if the thinking was "If we're responsible for implementing the change, we are excused from making the change in ourselves."

2. Resistance to change is often resistance to the process of change rather than to the particular change at hand.

This, of course, had been my primary lesson learned on the tennis courts. When the change process was perceived, consciously or unconsciously, as coercive or manipulative, it generated resistance. When the coercion and judgment were taken out of the process, there was markedly less resistance. Yet corporate change tended to be driven by coercion and judgment. Just as on the tennis courts, the traditional approach was "Here's the model of how you should do it. Here's how you are doing it now. Here's what you should and shouldn't do to fit into this new model. And here are the consequences if you don't." Sadly, this is a very old, broadly established, and ineffective method for trying to ensure change.

3. Resistance to change within the corporation is rooted in the prevailing command-and-control corporate culture.

On the tennis courts, I had learned that there was a way to go about making changes that was fundamentally different from the accepted methodology generally practiced in the sports world. In the corporate world, that accepted methodology was called "command and control." Those in a position of authority attempted to control business results by giving commands to subordinates and "encouraging" compliance with them. This spawned resistance as well as inefficiency in coping with unanticipated situations. The question I asked myself and my clients was "Would the principles of awareness, choice, and trust (ACT) be a better method for attaining results?"

Before the ACT principles could be employed, I had to better understand how the existing forces in corporate culture interfered with the natural learning process of the individual. There was much to learn.

For example, I discovered that it was taken for granted at AT&T that each employee would think and act more or less alike. Their own term of endearment for this phenomenon was "the bell-shaped head." They joked about and accepted this bell-shaped mold as if it were an inevitable part of working for the company.

It was the way this giant company found uniformity and identity. Yet no one understood its rigid strength until the times changed and it became necessary to start thinking and behaving outside its boundaries. Suddenly "bell-shaped thinking" was recognized as the impediment that was constraining the growth of hundreds of thousands of individuals. In fact, bell-shaped thinking was becoming the greatest single barrier to AT&T's success·in the new competitive environment. Perhaps for the first time in corporate history a large company had to face the reality that its corporate culture was a barrier to its success. Despite this realization, however, AT&T executives found it almost impossible to stand sufficiently outside the culture they were a part of to understand it and change it. So they hired senior managers from other companies who were not so imbued in bell-shaped thinking. Archie McGill, from IBM, was one of them. But though McGill was free of the kind of micromanagement style practiced at AT&T, he was a product of IBM's command-and-control culture.

The forces of corporate culture are very strong and hard to recognize, and thus hard to change. Even though brilliant and complex schemes of reorganization and reengineering were conceived, AT&T inevitably ran up against unseen cultural patterns that governed how people thought and behaved. The result would inevitably be significant disruption in the internal dialogues of individual workers, amounting to resistance to the prescribed changes.

Understanding Resistance to Corporate Change

It was clear to me from my work with coaching that the distinction between Self 1 and Self 2 was critical to understanding self-interference. The internal environment in which the performance and learning took place made the biggest difference in the ability of a person to access and express potential. When this internal environment was dominated by the judgmental, overcontrolling, self-doubting voice of Self 1, then much less of Self 2's potential was available to perform at its best or achieve results. In most individual sports, there is only one Self 1 to cope with. In business, however, where there is so much direct interaction with co-workers and customers, more than one Self 1 is usually involved. Thus the possibilities for interference are multiplied.

Take a team that is working together on a project. Member A, trying to impress the others, presents a certain idea for improving a work process. The Self 1 of team member B becomes competitive because the process being improved was his brainchild. So B finds grounds to put down A's new idea. A debate ensues. Member C's Self 1 hates conflict, so C withdraws from the conversation. Member A interprets C's disinterest as nonapproval of his original idea, so he begins to doubt himself. Member D, thinking that the conversation is not progressing toward fruitful results, comes up with an idea that is inferior to A's and to the current process, but it prevails because it avoids a loss of face on the part of A or C.

A work team that can synchronize the combined strengths of the Self 2 capabilities of its members can produce results that far surpass what those individuals could accomplish working separately. At the same time, the combined Self 1's of a team can play off each other in such a way as to make the team far *less* effective. Thus teams that have learned to work effectively together regularly make better decisions and come up with superior solutions to those that could be made by the brightest individual on that team. And, sad to say, teams who have not learned to control their Self 1's regularly settle for solutions and decisions that would have been unacceptable to any of the individuals working alone.

The Work Environment: Three Conversations

The environment in which we work has a huge impact on how productive and satisfying our work will be. Traditionally, people have thought of work environments merely in terms of physical surroundings. Studies were done in many companies to determine the impact of the physical environment on productivity and morale. Would changes in lighting, architecture, or ambient music improve the quality of work? The external environment certainly does matter, but the Inner Game suggests that there is an even more important environment in which we work—the environment between our own ears. Our thoughts, feelings, values, assumptions, definitions, attitudes, desires, and emotions all contribute to this internal environment.

Like a weather system, the inner environment has a great range of climatic conditions. When the weather is clear, you can see forever. Goals, obstacles, and critical variables for success are seen distinctly, and work can proceed in a cohesive and fulfilling way. But when the winds of internal conflict are gusting, thoughts and feelings are pulling us in different directions, and it's easy to lose all perspective. Priorities become confused, commitments are compromised, and doubts, fears, and self-limitations rule.

This inner work environment does not exist in a vacuum. It is greatly affected by our communications with the people we are working with. The quality of our relationships and the resulting conversations with co-workers have a decisive impact on the way we think and feel while working. For example, a feeling of insecurity in a boss might lead him to overcontrol the team that works for him. As a consequence, the inner conversation of the team managers will involve diminished self-confidence, which in turn will inhibit both individual and team performance.

A less obvious conversation also has a great impact on work. It is the cultural conversation that takes place in the background of all communications at work. In the corporate world, this is called corporate culture, and it arises from the patterns of language, assumptions, expectations, and practices that have been established as the unwritten norms adhered to by the people working in that culture. Recently there has been a growing awareness of the great impact of these norms on the character and quality of our work. For example, one corporate culture may establish the norm that not rocking the boat is more important than taking a prudent risk. This norm probably hasn't been officially proclaimed, yet it can be

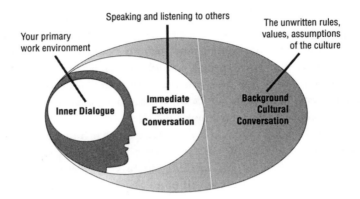

very hard to change. In some corporate cultures, questioning one's manager is totally unacceptable, while in another culture it is quite commonplace.

Let's look at each of these conversations a little more closely.

1. The Internal Conversation—There are many ways of allowing your thinking to get in the way of your performance and learning, but they all amount to conversations you are having with yourself within your own head.

Where does Self 1 interference come from and why is it there in the first place? I don't know the full answer to that question, but I know it has something to do with being human. It may have to do with the fact that we have a greater range of choice, of thought, and of language than other living creatures. I sometimes think of my Self 1 as an alien in me. This alien pretends to be me, but it is in fact the voice of *those other than me* that I have unconsciously incorporated into my internal dialogue. This voice, which may or may not have a separate agenda, establishes expectations, issues commands, and attempts to define my reality as if it were my boss. This invented self, which is derived from sources outside me, sows doubts that undermine my sense of wholeness, autonomy, and adequacy as an individual. From self-doubt arise the fears, judgments, overcontrols, and internal conflicts that disrupt the inner environment in which I work. Sometimes this voice sounds suspiciously like a parent, a teacher, a boss, or friends who want me to conform to various norms of my society.

I call Self 1 an alien voice not because its content is always false or harmful, but because it wants me (Self 2) to accept its dictates independent of my own direct experience or understanding. The tennis player who knew he took his backswing too high only because he had been told so by several pros, had little power to change because his error was not a matter of his direct experience and understanding. An outstanding literary example of Self 1 alienation is Huckleberry Finn, Mark Twain's protagonist, who experienced the conflict of a "guilty conscience" after realizing he was feeling respect and admiration for the runaway slave Jim. His entire culture had taught him to believe that black people were inferior, but his direct experience was telling him otherwise. In this case, Huck Finn had the courage to disregard the conditioned voice of his Self 1 and to follow the instincts and understanding of his Self 2.

The origin of Self 1 is not as important to me as the ability to distinguish it from the voice of my true self. Listening for and learning to trust the prompting of Self 2, the innate or natural self, is an essential and consistent challenge of the Inner Game. A harmonious relationship with oneself requires an internal conversation based in as much clarity, trust, and choice as possible. When people work in a group, there needs to be not only harmony with each individual, but aligned perceptions, aligned goals, and mutual trust among the group members.

2. The Immediate External Conversation—If the goal of the Inner Game is to quiet Self 1 interference so that Self 2 can be more fully expressed, another person can either help or hinder the process. As a coach, the way I speak to and relate to the student would either augment Self 1's disruption or facilitate Self 2's natural functioning.

Inner Game coaching works by introducing a different kind of

conversation from the one being carried on by Self 1. In the place
of judgmental observation, there is objective observation. In the
place of manipulation, there is choice. In the place of doubt and
overcontrol, there is trust in Self 2. When this external conversation changes in this way, it has a very real impact on the internal
environment of the player. Evidence of this lies in changes in facial
expression and smoother and more effective movement, as well as
much-improved results. Sometimes the change is instantaneous.
Often it goes back and forth with the flux of the player's internal
state of mind. The art and practice of having a beneficial impact
on the student's internal conversation have become my primary
quests as coach. The goal is to shift from a disruptive, confused,
and self-critical state of mind to one that is focused.

In the workplace, it is apparent that people working together
can either excite Self 1 doubts and fears or quiet them. If a worker
is viewed by one or more fellow workers as being less than competent, it tends to reinforce self-doubt, increase self-interference
with the worker's potential, and thus create a self-fulfilling proph-
ecy for all who are looking for and expecting to find the perceived
deficiency. Similarly, in a work team where the individual members view one another in mutual respect, encourage appropriate
risk taking, and value one another's capabilities, the internal dialogue has less of a chance to interfere, and workers perform better
than when alone.

3. The Cultural Conversation—Some corporate cultures are fear
based. People act primarily out of fear of being judged or punished. In a fear-based culture, the desire to look good—or not to
look bad—can take precedence over the business objectives at
hand and be the hidden driving force in conversations and meetings among co-workers. Other cultures are more obsessed with
control and power. The cultural conversations behind the work
conversations are characterized by who is in control, who is the
top dog, and who is the underdog. These conversations, though
often invisible to people in the culture, have great influence on

how the workers communicate with one another, and consequently on the internal environment of workers, producing many of the pressures and conflicts they experience as "normal" working conditions.

It was the recognition of the relationships between the three conversations—the internal, the immediate external, and the underlying cultural conversation—that allowed me to apply the Inner Game to a variety of activities at AT&T. The internal conversation within the worker was not all of his own making, but changed dramatically according to the quality of the surrounding cultural conversation. This in turn could have a huge impact on the worker's ability to produce results, make changes, and enjoy the process. To accomplish the optimal internal conversation, you must therefore become aware of yourself, aware of your co-workers, and, most challenging, aware of the cultural waters in which you are swimming.

Working Within Ma Bell's Culture

If I were to choose a single word to describe the cultural conversation in the background at AT&T, it would be *security.* I asked hundreds of people at various levels why they worked for the company. Underneath the surface diversity of the responses was one dominant motivation: job security. When I asked employees about the fundamental "deal" that they had with the company, the answer was quite uniform. "The deal is, if we come to work on time, do what is expected of us, and keep our noses clean, we are part of the family and will have a job for life." Loyalty to the company was the highest cultural value espoused. And loyalty was defined in terms not only of "how things are done around here," but also of "how we think around here." The practices and processes were well established and well communicated, and if you wanted to keep your job, you didn't question them. It was basically management by procedure. And it was pervasive.

The extent of this rigid form of management was driven

home to me one day as I was standing in an executive office of the Operator Services division in the corporate headquarters in Basking Ridge, New Jersey. Bragging about his degree of organization and managerial control, the executive asked me if I thought he knew what was happening in every telephone operator office across the country at that very moment. I raised my eyebrows. He pulled out one volume of a huge set in his office bookcase. He looked at his watch as he thumbed through the pages. "Here it is," he said as he began to read from the book of practices and procedures. "Right now the first-level supervisors should be having one-on-one feedback conversations about courtesy. They should at this time be talking about point number four. . . ." To prove it, he picked up the phone and called an office in Burbank, California, got the first-level supervisor on the phone, and asked what she was just doing. In a rather robotic voice, the supervisor described almost to the word how she was talking about point number four with a certain directory assistance operator. I found this chillingly impressive. The executive smiled and then turned to me and said, "But I think we can do even better. I want to know if the Inner Game could help us achieve higher levels of courtesy on our independent audits."

My feelings about accepting this invitation were mixed. In spite of the cumbersomeness of the bureaucracy and the obviously robotic mentality that it produced, AT&T's system was considered the best in the world at providing telephone service. Of course, it didn't have the constraint of having to be profitable by its own efforts. When expenses exceeded income, it was necessary only to ask a government commission to raise tolls. Without competition there was no big problem. But this protected culture was demolished when the Supreme Court ruled that AT&T would have to break up its monopoly. With that decision, the door was open to a highly competitive telecommunications industry in the private sector. As a result, what had been known as the Bell System was split apart, and AT&T managers had to begin to learn a whole new way of doing business based on the rules of a competitive marketplace. Massive changes in organizational structure and managerial practices were called for. Yet few of the existing managers felt confident that they knew how to facilitate such changes, since the challenge was to change the very way in which they made changes.

From the point of view of hundreds of thousands of employees, the change was perceived as a threat to their job security and as a fundamental betrayal of the original conditions of their employment. They had signed up to play a relatively safe game called "extended family" and were suddenly being required to play the risky game "competitive free enterprise." They hadn't signed up for this game, with its new rules, new values, and relative lack of security. Suddenly it was possible to be fired for no better reason than the company needed fewer people or one's performance results did not measure up to those of a fellow worker. It was as unthinkable as telling a teenager that he would be kicked out of the family if he didn't maintain a B average at school.

As it slowly dawned on Bell employees at all levels that their membership in the "family" was conditional upon meeting performance standards and not just "good behavior," it understandably produced significant turmoil in their inner environments. For those whose sense of self was dependent on the secure and nurturing embrace of Ma Bell, the new competitive culture was devastating.

It became hard to focus on work. The threat of job loss threw some workers into an even more desperate attempt to follow procedure correctly. While they soon learned the new language of competition and entrepreneurial management, it was hard to get beyond the language. One day a vice president in Operator Services complained to me, "We've been telling everyone for the past two months that they should think creatively and be willing to take more risks, but no one is doing it, even though we've assured them they won't be punished for mistakes." The compliance and management by procedures that were used for decades to mold the "bell-shaped head" were impotent to inspire the necessary entrepreneurial thinking and creative initiative. Workers were still in the mind-set of wanting to be told what to do and how to do it.

One can only imagine the impact on their internal conversations of this profound break in the social contract between them and their company. When a person's basic security is in doubt, most everything that happens seems threatening. All doubts find fertile ground. Motivation, focus, and trust evaporate. Individual, team, and corporate productivity suffer greatly as a consequence. Only those whose security was not so dependent on the old culture and who could access their own inner resources could make the choices necessary to achieve stability. Ironically, the individuals who had resisted compliance to the norms of the old culture were now the most valuable people to help the company survive its present crisis.

Most managers had little skill in coping with their own inner turmoil and certainly were not experienced in coaching others through it. All they knew was that they had to enforce higher standards and get better results than ever before. They themselves were as fearful of failure as the people they managed.

The Inner Game of Operating

The broad banner across the lobby of AT&T's Basking Ridge headquarters read CUSTOMER SATISFACTION. This was the slogan chosen to represent the new direction for all employees. Most managers had read Tom Peters's *In Search of Excellence* and other books saying that in the new market-driven business environment, the customer must be treated as king. Telephone operators, having direct contact with millions of customers, were on the front line of this new campaign. But how the customers were to be satisfied by operators who themselves were so dissatisfied in their work environment was not part of the conversation.

Working in an environment that offered little choice or opportunity, these operators could do little that was not written in the manual of procedures. Suddenly they were being asked to meet higher standards of performance. The normal reaction of operators was to shut down into themselves and become robotic. It was easy to hear the mechanical tone of voice that resulted.

My task was to design a training program that would result in measurable improvement in the "courtesy ratings" of these operators. Every telephone operator across the nation was rated according to courtesy, accuracy, and productivity. *Productivity* was another word for *speed*. "If we can shave another second off the average length of time the operator spends with the customer, we save the company millions of dollars," I was told with great enthusiasm. But the primary result they wanted from the Inner Game intervention was the improvement of courtesy ratings of the operators, as gathered and measured by external auditors. "In no case can the current average time per call be allowed to increase as a result of your training," I was informed.

As I considered what it was like to do the work of a telephone operator in the Bell culture, what stood out was the challenge of overcoming the boredom associated with the routine nature of the work: eight hours a day, five days a week, handling routine requests for directory assistance within the allotted average of 26.3 seconds per call.

I was fascinated by this challenge of overcoming boredom in routine work because it was an obstacle faced by millions—yet it had been largely unaddressed. However, I had two conditions. The first was that no operators would be *required* to attend the six hours of Inner Game seminar work. Participation in the training *and* the use of Inner Game tools were to be entirely voluntary. The second condition was that the Inner Game training would not have to be on the subject of courtesy.

So, on that basis, I was given a contract to produce a pilot program for the operators in the Burbank district in Southern California. If it worked, it was to be extended to other California districts within Pacific Telesis and then beyond. The application had to be simple enough to be communicated in three two-hour sessions and in a way that could be used by thousands of operators with whom I would have no direct contact.

The traditional approach would have been obvious: Research

the cutting-edge practices of customer courtesy, and produce a video of the ABCs of courtesy for telephone operators dramatizing the shoulds and shouldn'ts of operator courtesy. In other words, create the "mold" for the operators to fit themselves into. Then design a training program for the supervisors to observe the new operator behaviors and give feedback. Those falling short of the new standards would be identified and taken aside for private "coaching."

At best, such a program would have some impact on courtesy ratings over the short term, but without question it would not be appreciated by either the operators or their supervisors, who would see it as one more mold to fit into. Even if some new behaviors emerged, they would be as stilted and mechanical as those of a tennis player given the fourteen elements of the correct backhand. The AT&T training department had designed and implemented thousands of such programs and were much better at it than I would be.

So I decided on a different approach. It did not start from the premise that operators lacked knowledge of courtesy. Instead, it assumed that if Self 1's internal interference was reduced, more of Self 2's courtesy would be expressed as a natural consequence.

My first task was to observe the operators at work, set up interviews with some of them to find out how they viewed their work, and identify the major internal obstacles. The picture became clear quite quickly. (1) Most operators were bored and were doing their jobs very mechanically. One operator put it this way: "After the first six weeks, there's nothing more to learn on this job. We've heard all the problems and know how to handle them. I could do the job in my sleep, and sometimes that's just how it feels." (2) In spite of the boredom, there was a lot of stress on the job because operator productivity was monitored and measured closely and constantly. Office averages were posted regularly and individuals were given their daily average time per call at the end of each day. When it exceeded office levels, they were given "constructive feedback." (3) Operators felt they were treated like kids in elementary school by the system and by their supervisors. They were required to follow prescribed routines in all aspects of their work and to get permission for everything else, including going to the bathroom. Everything was justified by the necessity for higher productivity, accuracy, and courtesy. There was a lot of discontent with their jobs and hostility toward management. These conditions produced a disgruntled internal dialogue for the operators that expressed itself in conversations with customers that ranged from mechanical to irritated. Courtesy was not apt to be prominent.

I worked with a small team of colleagues to design a pilot training program that had nothing to do with courtesy. Instead, the goals were to reduce stress, reduce boredom, and increase enjoyment, which we hoped to accomplish by creating within each operator the attitude of a learner actively engaged in a learning process of his own choice. But how to make a routine job into an interesting learning environment? This turned out to be easier than it might seem.

We asked the operators what they could learn while doing their work. The unanimous response was, "Not much after the first few weeks."

We asked, "But what if your learning wasn't confined simply to doing a better job on courtesy, accuracy, and productivity [their three outer game goals, referred to as CAP]?" "Like what?" they asked. "Like learning not to be bored or not to be stressed, or learning to find enjoyment during the eight hours you are working." Some of the operators were openly skeptical. I found myself explaining that I had in fact been hired to have a positive impact on CAP, but that this was not the goal of the training. "This is a volunteer program for reducing stress and boredom in this job. You don't have to take it and you don't have to practice what is taught. But I expect that you will find it at least as much fun as your regular work." In the end, there was 100 percent sign-up.

We started by looking at the basic events of telephone operating. A light on the computer console would signal an incoming call, a customer would say something, the operator would punch information into the console and say something back to the customer. "What's the most interesting thing going on here?" I asked. Clearly it was the voice of the customer and the responding voice of the operator. I asked, "What can be learned besides mere data by listening to the customer's voice?"

Quite a bit could be learned if you listened. Even if a person were merely reciting a phone number, you might hear different levels of stress, how much of a hurry the person was in, what was going on in the background. "But what does that have to do with doing our job?" the operators asked. My answer was "Maybe nothing, but it might be an interesting experiment to find out how much you can tell about a person by listening to the tone of his voice and for any background sounds."

We invented a series of "awareness exercises" that called for operators to listen more closely to customers than they ever had before. It was like teaching tennis students to see more in the flight of a tennis ball. We asked the operators to rate on a scale of one to ten the various qualities they could hear in the customer's voice, like the degree of "warmth," "friendliness," or "irritation."

The next step was for the operators to learn to express different qualities in their own voices. It was like an acting class, and it was fun. When these two awareness exercises were put together, it became quite an interesting game. The operator would hear a stress level of nine come over her earphones. She might choose to give the response with a nine degree of warmth. More often than not, there would be a significant decrease in the stress in the customer's voice at the "good-bye."

The operators began to see that by choosing to express different qualities in their voices, they could have an impact on how they felt as well as on how the customer felt. Operators spoke with more than seven hundred people a day, and even though the conversations were short and confined, they could have a small but tangible impact on a great number of people.

How did this exercise reduce stress? Much stress came from irritated customers. But the operators found that when they were trying to listen closely to the customer to determine whether he was at a seven or eight irritation level, they didn't take the irritation to heart. The nonjudgmental awareness took the threat out of the irritated voice and elicited a wider range of positive responses.

As in tennis, the internal interference was reduced by higher levels of observation of what was happening in the immediate environment. The game was fun and self-reinforcing. And it didn't require supervisors to make sure it was being practiced. The operators used it at their discretion, and continued to use it, according to their own reports, off the job as well as on. It soon dawned on many that they could use these new listening skills in their close relationships with family members and friends. When the external measures of courtesy came, everyone involved was impressed. Courtesy ratings were improved beyond the expectations of management in spite of the fact that the operators were not trying to be more courteous. Operators were learning to listen and to express more of themselves. They were having more fun. It was quite obvious that operators who sounded more like human beings and not like bored robots would be perceived as more courteous by outside observers. And they were. I had learned to anticipate such indirect results. Others saw it as some kind of magic.

Meanwhile, the operators reported that levels of boredom and stress went down an average of 40 percent. Enjoyment on the job went up by 30 percent. The important lesson was that these subjective factors were much more in their control than they had thought. Before, operating was simply a dull, uninteresting job. Now they could change the quality of their work experience. Not being required to use these skills made them feel even more in control and left no opportunity for resistance.

Interestingly, the only negativity about the project came from supervisors. Because initiative had been left entirely in the hands of operators, some supervisors felt left out of the process, and thus left out of the credit for the results. From this, I learned a lot about how competition for credit in the corporate environment can threaten effective change initiatives. Adjustments had to be made to involve the supervisors in the training while still protecting the free choice of operators. Eventually, "The Inner Game of Operating" was packaged and delivered to nearly twenty thousand telephone operators in four regions of the country.

This experience left a profound impression on me. I saw the simple principles I had observed on the tennis courts produce measurable results in the workplace. I saw them make a huge difference to thousands of operators who thought they were confined to the boredom and stress of routine work done under pressure. I understood that even when a job was routine and could be done with only a small fraction of one's attention, there was a big payoff to the worker who would give the task his full attention. Even if heightened awareness wasn't necessary, it was beneficial to be as fully engaged as possible. Most important, I began to understand that the growth and development of the person doing the work was the most important work being done. This understanding became the foundation for all future work of the Inner Game.

Keeping Open to Self 2

The forces inhibiting Self 2 in the modern corporate culture are powerful and not to be underestimated. A few of the offices that implemented "The Inner Game of Operating" made the process mandatory and put supervisors in charge of making it happen. Of course, the magic went out of the program, courtesy did not improve, and justification was found for halting the program. The desire of management to ride herd on the behaviors of those below them was not an easy force to overcome. Many times it superseded the desire for results.

People are put into roles and told to follow procedures in the name of what is good for the corporation. Scripts are written and obeyed. The entire drama is being directed on a stage, but no one is quite sure who the director is. The saddest part is that having identified with their scripts, employees internalize the characters they have been asked to portray. Self 2, the self that is born with the gifts of freedom and self-expression, can easily be forgotten in the drama of the play.

I ran across a quote recently that puts it quite well:

> *There is a vitality, a life force, a quickening that is translated through you into action, and because there is only one of you in all time, this expression is unique. And if you block it, it will never exist through any other medium and be lost. The world will not have it. It is not your business to determine how good it is, nor how valuable it is, nor how it compares with other expressions. It is your business to keep it yours clearly and directly, to keep the channel open. You do not even have to believe in yourself or your work. You have to keep yourself open and aware directly to the urges that motivate you. Keep the channel open.*[*]

The goal to work freely while maintaining the integrity of Self 2 is a challenging one. It requires great control over the factors that influence one's inner environment. This in turn requires an increased awareness of and independence from the surrounding cultural conversation, as well as more conscious communication with one's co-workers. Work culture can be changed only through the interactions between co-workers.

Any manager or coach of a team can make a significant difference in the interactions between individuals of that team. This can minimize the amount of self-interference and increase the team's access to their collective capabilities to learn and perform. Furthermore, corporate leaders who recognize the far-reaching implications of the corporate culture are in a position to learn how to identify the important levers of cultural change. The goal is to make changes in organizational culture that minimize self-interference and acknowledge the inherent motivations and talents of the work force.

But cultural patterns tend to change slowly—too slowly for

---

[*] Martha Graham to biographer Agnes de Mille in *Martha: The Life and Work of Martha Graham* (New York: Random House, 1992).

the individual worker to count on meaningful change in the short term. My hope for working free cannot rest on external changes, but on whatever I can do to optimize my internal work environment. As everyone who has excelled in any sport knows, winning in the long term is largely a function of one's state of mind. State of mind—the inner environment—is in turn a function of a person's ability to attain and sustain *focus*.

The rest of this book is about the quest to allow more and more of Self 2 potential to be available to both the individual at work and the work group.

3

FOCUS
OF
ATTENTION

"Our acts of voluntary attending, as brief and fitful as they are, are nevertheless momentous and critical, determining us, as they do, to higher or lower destinies.

—William James

If there is one thing that excellence in sports and excellence in work have in common, it can be summed up in a single phrase: *focus of attention*. Focus is the quintessential component of superior performance in every activity, no matter what the level of skill or the age of the performer.

The simple fact is that we do our best when we are focused, whether we are riding a bicycle, drawing a plan for a suspension bridge, conceiving a global strategy for a multinational company, negotiating a contract, selling a product, cutting sushi, tasting a glass of wine, appreciating a sunset, throwing a ball, or writing a book. And when focus is lost, we simply do not perform at our best.

Children focus. Animals focus. Adults focus. It's a primary ability of living creatures—perhaps even built into the DNA as a necessity for natural selection. Of all these, adults seem to have the most difficulty with focus. Children may have short attention spans but do not get easily distracted from what is important to them. One could say that most of the mistakes made by adults are caused by a loss of focus of attention. And with that loss of focus comes a loss of productivity, learning, and enjoyment in the process of work.

It is by focus of attention that we make contact with everything in our world and by this means alone that things become knowable and understandable to us. Thus, attention is critical to all learning, understanding, and proficiency of action. It is only when we are giving our full attention to what we are doing that we can bring all of our resources to bear effectively. Why? Because when we are giving full attention, self-interference is neutralized. In the fullness of focus, there is no room for Self 1's fears or doubts.

Self 2 Focus

When I first discovered the power of simple focus of attention on the tennis courts, it was so compelling that I believed it to be critical to success in all things, and I thought it to be the master skill behind all skill development. Athletes often call it "playing in the zone." I like to call it Self 2 focus. When we experience this kind of focus, excellence in performance seems to happen magically, almost effortlessly. If we could learn to understand the nature of this kind of full attention, we would be able to perform much better in whatever we do, learn faster and more comprehensively, and enjoy ourselves much more in the process.

First, it should be pointed out that Self 2 focus is not achieved by self-discipline alone. Trying too hard to concentrate produces a constrained and forced focus that is difficult and tiring to sustain. It is not inherently enjoyable, and in the long term, it is simply not effective.

For example, have you ever been confronted with a salesperson who has recently been instructed to "maintain eye contact with the customer"? It has the opposite of the intended effect. Instead of making you feel more contact with and trust in the salesperson, you feel uncomfortable and defensive. The difference between that forced attention and spontaneous interest may be hard to describe, but it is immediately apparent.

If you observe the focus of a young child playing or of a cat following a fly with its eyes, you are seeing Self 2 focus. The critical element is the clarity of desire behind the focus. The cat is fascinated by the fly and the child wants to be playing. Desire focuses attention. When one is connected with one's own desire, Self 2 focus occurs naturally. But when desire is missing or one is subject to conflicting desires, then one is apt to feel that it is necessary to "fight" to stay focused. Then the internal commands start, saying, "Keep your eye on the ball" . . . or the page . . . or the person.

Self 1 Distractions

Self 2 focus is not hard to demonstrate. Coaching a tennis player, I might give the following instruction: "As the ball comes toward you, I want you to notice anything about its trajectory that interests you." I might follow up with a few questions to encourage even greater focus on the specific details the player reports finding interest in. As more and more focus is given to the ball, there will be a noticeable improvement in the quality of the tennis performance. If an audience is watching, I will often ask them how they explain the improved performance given the absence of any performance-related instructions. The most common response to this question is, "You distracted him."

"What did I distract him from?" I ask.

The answer comes: "You distracted him from thinking so much about how he should hit the ball. You distracted him from worrying about the results."

In short, what becomes evident is that focus is what distracts us from whatever is distracting us. If all the internal dialogue about results and about technique were actually helpful, then performance would not have improved. But the internal dialogue is not helpful. It simply distracts you from the needed effort.

Recently, I asked a manager I was coaching, "What contributes to your focus while working and what distracts you?" His initial reply was, "When I am enjoying what I do, my focus tends to be deeper; when I am doing what I have to do but don't really want to do, my focus is more easily distracted." This brings up an essential point about focus. Focus is easier to sustain when you are doing something you have freely chosen to do. In this sense focus is not a skill you develop by learning a technique. It is more a function of your motivations being lined up behind what you are doing. A teenager might find it very easy to focus while on the basketball court but almost impossible in the classroom while studying English grammar. Likewise, an employee who hasn't "bought into" the purpose behind a particular assignment will find it more difficult to focus attention than an employee who understands the importance of the task and feels fully aligned with it. So interest, motivation, and choice all have a great deal to do with one's ability to focus deeply and to sustain that focus over long periods of time. Focus feels very good, and the work that comes from a focused mind is generally good work.

My next question to the manager was, "What distracts focus while working?"

He replied, "The telephone, other people, distracting sounds and sights." I delved deeper, asking, "But if you are alone working on a project and there are no external distractions, is your focus consistent, or is it better sometimes than others?"

The manager thought for a while and said, "There is definitely a wide range in my focus day to day, even hour to hour. I suppose one variable has to do with what else is on my mind at the time. If I have an unresolved issue from another project, or at home, then thoughts about that issue can come in and distract me from what I'm doing. In fact, I often have different agendas competing for my attention all at the same time. I focus best when I can come to a project without any issues brought from the past and am ready to give my full attention to it."

Competing agendas is an apt phrase to describe the source of distraction. From my observations, Self 2 usually has a very simple agenda. It wants to focus on whatever will fulfill its innate goals.

When Self 2 isn't interfered with by Self 1, it expresses its desire with an elegant economy of effort. But when Self 2 cannot resolve the competing agendas of Self 1 and various external forces, focus will be elusive. The desire to communicate to another or to resolve an issue at work is very different from the desire to avoid making a mistake, or the desire to gain credit for the result. Though both Self 1 and Self 2 might want the same outcomes, the Self 1 desire generated by doubt or fear is very different from the natural desire to enjoy the expression of one's capabilities. In short, Self 1's doubt-and-fear-based agendas compete with the simple agendas of Self 2. We attain a natural and relaxed focus when our interest is absorbed in the task at hand, connected with our true motivations, and we are able to disregard the distractions generated by the Self 1 "other in us."

When Self 2 focus is occurring, it seems magical because the actions are more spontaneous and unexpectedly effortless. Self-consciousness is gone. Self-judgment is gone. The overcontrolling mechanisms of fear and doubt are gone. When this kind of focus is happening, there is neither anxiety nor boredom. In their place is a simple state, not easily described, but inherently enjoyable, often surprising, and creative—even during repetitive activities. Within such a focus, a rhythm and an effortlessness develop that one finds pleasing and satisfying.

Mihaly Csikszentmihalyi, in his seminal book about the experience of play and work, *Beyond Boredom and Anxiety,* refers to it as the *flow state.* He describes it as follows:

> *In the flow state, action follows upon action according to an internal logic that seems to need no conscious intervention by the actor. He experiences it as a unified flowing from one moment to the next, in which he is in control of his actions, and in which there is little distinction between self and environment, between stimulus and response, or between past, present, and future.*

A wonderful example of this kind of Self 2 focus is Michelle Kwan's performance in ice skating championships. She and other top skaters capture in their performance the ease and elegance that can result from this kind of focus even when surrounded by the pressures of topflight competition. The difference between her and lesser skaters is apparent not in technical merit alone, but in the integration of her desire, her capability, and her inner joy expressed in action. And what grasps the audience is not just the high level of achievement, but the total lack of self-interference that makes her talent and qualities visible.

Yet the focus can be the same even at lower levels of skill. When teaching tennis, it was my common and universal experience that if the student could bring full attention to bear on a tennis ball in enough detail, it would distract him from the thoughts that originated in doubt and fear. With interference and overcontrol out of the way, the student hits the ball better and natural enjoyment emerges. Improvement in technique and development of skill happen automatically.

The ACT Δ and Self 2 Focus

What I had learned on the tennis courts was that there are three essential contributors to Self 2 focus: awareness, choice, and trust. These same elements are what contribute to focus in the performance of any work task.

Awareness: The *Light* of Focused Attention—Awareness is like light. Whatever it shines on becomes knowable and potentially understandable. Just as focused light brings objects into greater defini-

tion and clarity, so *focus of attention* brings clarity and distinctness to whatever is being observed. When focus is broad, an entire landscape can be viewed; when it is narrow, one can see the detail of a particular leaf on a tree in that landscape. It is even possible to focus on the single leaf in the foreground of one's attention while retaining awareness of the larger landscape in the background.

Through focused awareness our world becomes understandable. Superficial understanding will arise when one has attended only to the surface of things. Profound understanding requires attending to what lies beneath the visible surface. Likewise, the comprehensiveness of our understanding of any situation or subject depends on the attention given to all its relevant aspects and their relationship to each other. Thus the quality of our attention is linked to the quality of both one's learning and performance.

Errors in judgment are made when attention is paid in too narrow a range, resulting in what is commonly called "tunnel vision." This tunnel vision can occur within an individual or in a team of people working together. When the team's focus of attention becomes governed by the individual Self 1 agendas of its members, team focus is lost and its effectiveness compromised.

Choice and Focus—What is rarely appreciated about focus is that it is governed by desire. A pickpocket focuses on the purse or wallet; a lover is always looking toward the loved one. A person connected with his desire will notice whatever is critical to success. A trout fisherman does not have to "try to focus," but is intent on whatever may signal the presence of trout. The musician hears the variables that pertain to rhythm, melody, and tone. In the same way, a person in the grip of fear will notice whatever is frightening, and the angry person will notice whatever is making him angry. Desire drives focus. Our choice is over which desires to nourish and which to starve. Nourishing the natural desires of Self 2 builds stability and leads toward self-fulfillment. The nurturing of Self 1 desires strengthens self-interference and leads to inner conflict and distraction.

But where humans have desire, we also have choice. We have

the choice of which desires to nurture and which to starve. By our choices we create the priorities by which we act in this world. When we are clear about these priorities, focus is easier to come by. When we are unclear, our agendas are in conflict, our orientation becomes ambiguous, and focus is difficult to sustain.

Fundamentally, the choice is between Self 1 and Self 2. I can choose to be in touch with my own inherent priorities (Self 2) or I can be distracted from them by the internalized agendas that others have for me (Self 1). As I gain in my ability to make this distinction between my own voice and that of "the others in me," I can gain easier access to Self 2 focus. The choice is exercised every time I choose to focus my attention.

How Trust Contributes to Focus—This leads to the third element of focus. Why is trust critical to focus? Because it happens only when you let go of a certain kind of mental control. When Self 1 is in a state of doubt, the flow state is broken. This is when you are apt to hear instructions in your head about what you should or shouldn't do, or questions about every choice you make. Doubt leads to confusion and to paralysis of action. When you are focused, you are conscious of your purpose, fully engaged in the present, and the voice of Self 1 is not heard.

The more I can learn to trust Self 2, the less I am affected by fear and doubt and the easier it is to sustain focus. This letting go of control brings the magic to athletes, writers, and creative problem solvers. When my Self 1 is in control, I get Self 1 kinds of results. When Self 2 is allowed to do the action, spontaneously, something always happens that I would not have thought of, that is more elegant, simpler, truer. Whenever I see this, I am delighted, whether it is in me or in another person. It is beautiful.

The price of this beauty is that it cannot be controlled by conscious thought. It can only be allowed. This takes trust and a bit of humility. Humility is an important part of both focus and trust. Arrogance is thinking I know everything that is happening, so I think I do not have to pay much attention. If I trust myself to admit that I don't know everything, then I am more attentive and I will learn. I see things that I haven't seen in ways that I have not seen before. This freshness of perception is a sign that Self 2 is the one focusing attention and that the Self 1 "know-it-all" is quiet. It is scary to give up the Self 1 control you thought you needed. But you must trust that Self 2 will take over the control and it will do a better job.

Fighting Self 1 Does Not Work—When Self 2 focus occurs, there is a flow and rhythm to one's actions that is inherently satisfying. It seems that things are working at all levels. Performance generally flows smoothly and with economy of effort, learning is taking place naturally and spontaneously, and a good feeling is present. When we experience this state for a short time, it is natural to try to somehow keep it, or if we lose it, to *make* it return. We demand the return of spontaneity and flow. And it usually doesn't work. Why?

When I lose focus, I can be sure there is some conflict between Self 2 and Self 1. But what can I do about it? If I use Self 1 strategies to control Self 1, I will strengthen the very taskmaster that is causing the conflict. If I get caught up in resisting Self 1, the distractions will only get stronger. If I try to force my way into Self 2 focus, I will delay its return. If I tell Self 1 to shut up, it is likely to speak louder. Either giving in to Self 1 or fighting it directly is a losing battle.

So, what can I do? The only thing that works for me is to choose Self 2—to acknowledge its desire and allow it to express itself. How can I do this when I'm in conflict? If there is conflict, then I can be sure that Self 2 is there! If it were not, there wouldn't be any conflict. The resistance itself is evidence that Self 1 is not having its full sway over me. Once I can acknowledge Self 2, I can reach for it and give it whatever attention I have at my disposal. By that conscious choice I am ignoring the voices of self-interference. A little attention is withdrawn from Self 1, diminishing its influence, and I simultaneously gain greater access to the resources of Self 2.

The Practice of Ignoring Self 1—To dramatize this practice of focus, the following exercise was designed for use in any sales training. I ask A to sell B on doing some action—such as going to a movie, reading a book, going to a seminar, buying a stock. Then buyer and seller are each assigned a person to play the role of Self 1. The Self 1's instructions are simple: "Do whatever you can short of physical intervention to distract your partner from the task at hand." They are also told they can't speak in a voice above a whisper.

It's amazing how creative and subtle the Self 1's are in their strategies and techniques of distraction. "Look at him, I don't think he's buying what you are saying . . . maybe you should try something else. . . . Now that was a really smart thing to say . . . do you really believe that yourself? . . . You should try to find out his hot buttons. . . . She's resisting everything you're saying. . . . I don't think she likes you that well . . . well, why should she? . . . Why don't you try flirting a little? . . . Yes, that's much better . . . now you're getting somewhere . . . do you want some other ideas? . . ."

On the buyer's side, you can hear whispers such as "He's trying to put this over on you . . . he doesn't know what he's talking about . . . don't fall for that line. . . . Don't you think he's being a little condescending? . . . Don't get sucked into this. . . . You know, he thinks you are attracted to him . . . I think he's trying to flirt with you . . . can you imagine? . . . why not play along a bit? . . . Then stick it to him at the end and turn him down flat. . . ."

When the Self 1's are asked what they learned from the exercise, they are very clear about several things: (1) They are surprised at how good they are at their roles and realize that they must have been "practicing" this for a long time. (2) It is fun doing it on purpose and to someone else instead of themselves. (3) Self 1's can be either negative or positive. Whether they undermine confidence or build up ego, all they really have to do is to command a certain amount of the attention of their "victims."

The buyers and sellers learn similar lessons. At first, they don't know whether the whisperers are put there to help or not. (Just as it's usually hard to tell if the Self 1 whisper in your head is a friend or foe.) "Maybe they were told to be our coaches," some of them think. When the Self 1's play their roles well, and they usually do, it is quite a while before the buyers and sellers realize they are being distracted and try to protect themselves. Of course, if they try to pick a fight with their Self 1's by arguing, they always lose. It doesn't matter to the clever Self 1's if they are agreed with or argued with—in either case, they have succeeded in their goal of distracting the buyer or seller from his task. The only way for either buyer or seller to work effectively is to make a decision to tune out his Self 1. Those who make this choice find that they can effectively block out the Self 1 voices by giving full attention to the communication with the other person.

We all have our Self 1 whisperers. It helps to realize that we don't have to listen to them. Our Self 1's have the upper hand every time they can convince us either that we need their advice, or that we need to fight them into submission. In either case, they succeed in distracting us from the task at hand. Focus is thus the best defense and the best offense against Self 1 interference.

Creating an "Inner Environment" for Focus

Once you begin the practice of focus, the first thing you may learn is how easily you are distracted. This is a critical part of the practice of focus. What distracts you during work? Most people don't realize how scattered their attention is until they consciously attempt to learn to maintain focus. Maintaining focus is not a matter of never losing focus, but a matter of shortening the periods of time in which you lose focus. The best goal for learning focus is to become good at coming back.

Learn the warning signs of not being focused. Sometimes mistakes in performance reveal a momentary (or longer) lapse. I also lose focus more easily when I am anxious, bored, or confused. What prompts these feelings? Self 2 focus is generally a result of two conditions: sufficient safety and sufficient challenge. When a person experiences too much challenge and too little safety, he tends to become anxious or stressed. When a person experiences too little challenge and too much safety, he tends to become bored. In either case, focus is easy to lose.

Too Much Challenge, Not Enough Safety = Stress

—The experience of "too much demand" is one of the most common conditions for loss of focus. Almost everyone I have spoken to in corporate management works in the context of "I have more to do than time to do it in." Not only do all the demands clamor for attention at the same time, but the mere condition of feeling overwhelmed impairs focus. The key is to restore choice to the matter and ultimately alleviate the sense of overdemand.

One way to reduce "demand" is to get rid of the unnecessary demands of Self 1 in the form of such things as perfectionism, overcontrol, avoidance of risk, etc. Once you have eliminated all the Self 1 demands possible, if you still have more to do than time to do it, you can begin to look at how and why you accepted a larger load than you had time for and decide how to renegotiate or delegate some of the demand. One way to do this is to divide your time into thirds. What would you do if you only had a third of the time you actually have available? What would you do if you had only two-thirds? You should probably stop there, as the last third will be taken by tasks that would be impossible to anticipate.

In the final analysis, you can do work effectively only if you can stay focused, and you can't stay focused when feeling overburdened by too much demand. I am often surprised by how much time I save when I have let go of Self 1 demands and of my resistance to them. Self 1 likes to take all the time available to do a given task. Self 2 likes to do the task with economy of time and effort in keeping with purpose. When I get out of the Self 1 mode, Self 2 finds a pace for working that is in keeping with its nature. Without exception, work simply gets done more efficiently and effectively in keeping with purpose.

Too Little Challenge and Too Much Safety = Boredom

—When a person feels too *little* demand because a job or task is perceived as being too routine or unimportant, focus can be usurped by a sense of boredom. The cycle of boredom works very much like the cycle of anxiety described in the previous chapter. The perception "Nothing is interesting here" leads to a shutting down of receptors in the nervous system and a condition of nonalertness, an inability to stay interested, which leads to a lack of engagement in the activity, which leads to the conclusion that "this work is boring." The cycle continues.

Lack of challenge is as threatening to Self 2's well-being as too much challenge. Self 2 goes to sleep and a person often feels forced to look for extreme means of "excitement" and stimulation outside of work in order to feel alive again.

There are two solutions to this problem. Find a way to bring greater challenge into your existing work by raising the standards and paying greater attention to detail than necessary (like the telephone operators), or find more meaningful or challenging work. Sometimes boredom is an easier obstacle to overcome than anxiety, because more of the variables are in your control. One key is not to identify yourself with the work you are doing. Faced with "boring and routine work," you can still be a very interesting and important person. Likewise, you can be a very calm and collected person doing very stressful work. You owe it to yourself to take charge of your own inner environment and make the decision that you will not allow yourself to stay bored or stressed for long.

Regaining Lost Focus—I want to go for it . . . I don't want to fail. I know I can do it . . . I'm not so sure. I want the responsibility . . . I don't want the pressure. I want to learn to play the piano . . . I don't want to endure those tedious lessons. I want to be open to my feelings . . . I don't want to feel hurt. I'm willing to take the risk . . . I can't afford to be wrong. The instances of conflicted goals and desires can be endless. But they all amount to a lack of clarity about one's priorities. The resulting state is one of confusion in which sustained focus is improbable.

Distraction is a failure to resolve an inner conflict of priorities. We all live in worlds where there are many demands placed upon us. Parents, bosses, partners, managers, colleagues, teachers, governments, friends, religions, coaches, children—our "ideals" and causes all assume the right to "ask" things of us. Most of us feel the obligation to accommodate some or most of the agendas that others have for us—often to the neglect of Self 2's agenda.

What priority do we give to our inherent needs for balance, enjoyment, growth? To what extent do we allow ourselves to be a priority in our own lives? Some will consider such a thought selfish. Not true. Common sense dictates that if the cow doesn't get to eat grass, it won't have milk to give. If Self 2 isn't acknowledged and nourished, how much will it be able to give? It is the nature of society to create never-ending demands on all of us. Yet it is the nature of the human spirit to be free. The root of our inability to focus is this fundamental conflict between the individual and its surrounding society.

This choice is a simple one, but it is not always so easy to make. The first step is to distinguish the feel of Self 1's compulsive forces from the gentler urgings of Self 2. It is easier to feel the difference than it is to describe it. Self 1 desire feels as if I'm being driven by a tight hand at the wheel, Self 2 as if I'm doing the driving with a relaxed but firm grip. Self 2 is naturally joyous in its expression of its excellence; Self 1 is trying to prove itself or earn something it often doesn't think it really deserves. There are many descriptions, but none will replace the ability to distinguish how they feel from the inside.

When I don't know what I want, I fall prey to the agendas of Self 1. This is how Self 1 gets strong in the first place. Being socialized means following the agendas of "the other" at the expense of your own inherent guidance system. Self 2 focus occurs when such inner conflict has been resolved or when for the moment all desires are aligned in the same direction.

Choice and commitment are very powerful forces that are available to each one of us. Bringing choice beyond the level of what I am doing to include who or what I am following is not only a key contributor to focus, but the essential ingredient of individual freedom itself. There is no easy trick to staying focused. It takes awareness, choice, trust, and a lot of practice.

4

THE PRACTICE OF FOCUS

Focus is about paying attention while doing whatever you are doing. It is a skill that can be practiced through any activity—driving a car, reading a book, talking and listening to another person, solving a problem, tending a machine, working with others or working alone.

The most important thing about the practice of focus is that it cannot be forced. Trying hard to concentrate doesn't work. It produces frustration, tiredness, and narrowness of vision. Focus follows interest, and interest does not need coercion. A gentle hand on the steering wheel of attention will suffice.

A second thing to keep in mind about the practice of focus is to be nonjudgmental. When you practice staying focused you are apt to become more aware of your distractions. If you get angry with yourself for losing focus, you will compound your distraction from the task at hand. The alternative approach is that of the learner. As a learner, I want to maintain my focus, but I am also interested in identifying what distracts me.

When coaching a student to focus on the tennis ball, my primary effort was to encourage focus on some aspect of the flight of the ball that the student found interesting. When the focus of attention was lost I might ask, "Where did your attention go?" The student would reflect for a moment and then express surprise that his attention had gotten distracted as if without his permission. Just noticing what had pulled attention away was usually sufficient to weaken that distraction and allow for greater focus.

One should not conclude that all shifts in attention amount to a loss of focus. Self 2 will automatically shift attention when it finds something interesting and relevant to attend to. Only if I have learned to notice my shifts of attention can I tell when such a shift is contributing to my purpose or distracting from it.

When you are driving a car, your attention shifts many times in an effort to get all the information necessary to keep you safe and on course. Rather than hinder your ability to drive well, these shifts of attention are crucial to driving safely and they can even be used to enhance your focus and performance. For example, I once began to notice where on the road my eyes fell when driving around turns on a rural road. As I increased my focus, I noticed that my eyes started to find a place further from the beginning of the turn and more toward its completion. Focusing on that part of the turn made a marked improvement in the ease with which I negotiated the turn. Simply becoming aware of where your attention is will increase your focus.

Practicing focus means being fully aware and present to the variables that matter. As you notice what distracts you, your priorities become clarified and focus is strengthened. This is the heart of practicing the Inner Game in any activity. As focus increases, self-interference decreases, and performance inevitably improves.

Focused Communication—One of the most valuable areas at work in which to practice focus is in communicating with another person. Effective work involves good communication, and focus of attention is the critical element to effective communication. Again, start with nonjudgmental observation.

Have you ever noticed the extent to which there is a conversation going on in your head while you are talking with another person? I find that internal comments and feelings often distract me from fully listening to the other person. I find myself thinking

I already know what the person is going to say, so I don't really have to listen. I think about whether I agree or disagree with what is being said and I rehearse my next response. How much of my attention does this internal conversation absorb?

The task of listening to another person is not that different from that of focusing on a tennis ball. The other person's voice is coming toward you and you are going to have to respond. What are you thinking and feeling while the communication is coming your way? Do you feel like the tennis player who is threatened by a hard shot toward his backhand? "Here comes a judgment or rejection right toward my weakness"? Or, "Here comes a statement I don't agree with." Just as with the defensive tennis player, such a listener is subject to the cycle of self-interference. Shallow breathing, flushed face, tightened body posture, and other physiological reactions disrupt the harmony of the inner environment. The listener is apt to be thrown into a defensive posture that makes it just as hard for him to respond appropriately as it is for the tennis player to return a difficult shot.

What do I think would happen if I let go of my Self 1 control mechanisms and gave my full attention to the speaker? Do I really need to make comments to myself or rehearse my response while the other person is talking? When I am willing to listen more fully, the other person notices that attention is being paid and often starts speaking and listening in a more focused way. The result can be a general improvement in the quality of the communication both ways.

Listening and Speaking—Self 2 focus in listening and speaking cannot be accomplished by discipline alone. You have to let yourself get interested in the other person. And you can get interested only if you don't assume you already know what is being said. This can make you feel a little more open and vulnerable, but it is critical to Self 2 focus. When I can accept these feelings, I have more attention to give to both the content and the feelings of the other person. On the other hand, when I am not willing to be open and in a state of not knowing, I can become defensive, judgmental, anxious, or bored.

Let me offer one short example of the difference between Self 1 and Self 2 listening. I was in a meeting as a part of a small work group with an assigned task. In this group, there was a middle-aged manager who provoked my Self 1. Almost every time she spoke, it was to give advice to someone about something. If a person was expressing a concern or a problem, she would automatically come up with "Why don't you try doing it this way?" My Self 1 was commenting, "Advice when it's not asked for is just the kind of thing I hate. . . ." It was being as judgmental of her as it often is of myself. Of course, the more I focused on this annoying behavior, the less aware I was of the rest of the surrounding conversation in the work group, and the less able I was to make a contribution to the task at hand. Self 1's internal assessment was "This meeting is a total waste of time."

We broke for lunch and I got into a conversation with someone else from the group who had gotten a great deal out of the meeting. When I brought up how annoying this particular manager had been, he acknowledged that he had noticed the behavior, but had ignored it because he was interested in other things that were being said. "Besides, I know her, and in spite of the fact that she's a bit free with her advice, she is one of the most intelligent and compassionate managers around." I was shocked. It was as if we had been at two totally different meetings and were talking about two totally different people. I realized that the meeting I had been in was not one I wanted to return to and that I had a *choice*— not whether or not to return to the meeting, but *what I would listen for* while I was in the meeting. I made a simple choice—to listen for what I could appreciate in the work group rather than for what I could criticize.

Objectively speaking, very little was different in the meeting after lunch from the one that I had thought was a waste of time. But subjectively, I was in a totally different meeting. The behavior of the advice-giving manager did not change, but my view of her changed a lot. I could see that she was both intelligent and compassionate and in fact quite a wonderful manager. I still didn't like this particular behavior, but I was able to distinguish the person from her behavior. This made all the difference in how I saw her. Instead of seeing only the "pimple," I could see the whole face. From this perspective, I could also listen with better focus to the others in the group. To my surprise, I found that real work was happening, and found several chances to make my contribution to the effort. By the end of the meeting, I had to admit that this had been a productive meeting and probably had been all along.

It was a most valuable learning experience in the difference between Self 1 and Self 2 listening. It is easy to get caught in Self 1's critical frame of mind, which looks for evidence to justify one's preconceptions. What I seldom realize is that it may not be the other person who is wasting my time, but that I am wasting my own time by listening with such an attitude. The fact is that I have a choice in the matter, even though it is much more convenient to blame the other person, the meeting, or life itself.

It takes a lot of attention to really understand what is being said by another person. Even in the transfer of simple information, it has been well established by researchers that people generally don't hear what others are saying. We hear what we *expect* to hear. Compounding the problem, people often don't say what they really mean. Meaning can be disguised by the speaker's efforts to be polite, to avoid judgment, or to make a good impression. Picking up on what a person is really saying can require total focus on the part of the listener. Since our attention is directly related to our ability to understand, and understanding the people we work with is directly related to our ability to perform well (especially in teams), the value of learning to give full attention while listening is hard to overestimate.

The converse is also true. Speaking requires as much focus as listening. Do we say whatever comes into our minds whether it is relevant or not? Focus in speaking has to do with saying what you mean in a way that can be understood, respected, and considered relevant.

One of the reasons people don't like business meetings is that they can be so unfocused. Even with a pre-established agenda, what one person says often has absolutely nothing to do with what the previous person said. When this happens, you can safely assume that when the first person was speaking, the second person was thinking about whatever he was going to say next instead of listening. If one were to analyze the flow of such conversations in the workplace, it might be quite surprising to see how incoherent and seemingly random many of them are.

It is also difficult to maintain focus when the person speaking takes several minutes to say what could be said in a few seconds. In speaking, as in sports, Self 2 likes to express itself concisely.

Since communication is such a pervasive part of our lives, it affords an ideal opportunity to practice focus of attention every time we listen or speak.

Focus on Critical Variables

We make contact with and understand the world around us through our attention, which is constantly shifting according to our interest. In any activity, there are an unlimited number of possible objects of attention. It is the understanding that we bring to a situation that governs what objects of attention we will select. In turn, it is what we perceive through our attention that will govern our understanding. Thus, while understanding can grow with each focusing of attention, it can be eroded by the withdrawal or distraction of attention.

Self 2 is the inherent intelligence behind our selection of what to attend to. And Self 1 is the prime distracter of attention; it can erode focus and make us less conscious of where we are and where we are going. As Self 1 becomes still, Self 2 focus is allowed to emerge, and it naturally selects those objects that are most relevant. I call these "critical variables." In a conscious Self 2 state, these shifts of attention occur quite automatically and bring new information with each new observation. Understanding thus grows automatically, and from understanding come better choices and better performance.

Focus on speed—When it came time to teach my teenage son, Steve, how to drive, I did so almost entirely through the practice of focus of attention on critical variables. It started with playing informal "awareness games" while Steve was in the passenger seat. I would ask questions such as, "Is my car more in the right side of the lane, the left, or in the center?" Or "How many car lengths am I from the car in front of me, or the car behind me?" These questions were not about getting a correct answer, but were designed to increase Steve's awareness of distances and spaces.

A question like "How fast are we going?" does not provide an interesting opportunity for focus. So the game was to guess the car's speed without looking at the speedometer. We would each make a guess and then look at the speedometer to confirm. Then the question was, what did you observe in making your guess? We began to be aware of the *sub-variables* of the variable *speed*. The sounds of the engine, the wind on the windshield, or the wheels on the road all gave auditory information relevant to speed. The motion of the white lines, telephone poles, trees, and other stationary objects gave visual clues. Attending to these sensory clues made the driving lessons interesting and absorbing and, more important, it was about being aware and being accurate. It was not about making judgments of good or bad driving.

When it came time for Steve to get behind the wheel, the conversation continued to be nonjudgmental. We had a short conversation about the objective of driving—namely to get safely and legally from A to B. Once this objective was clearly stated, I began asking the awareness questions. The first few times I asked the questions, it was when Steve was driving well. We could ask and answer the questions in a neutral tone of voice. The nonjudgmental context made the learning progress rapidly, without criticisms. It was amazing to see just how aware Steve would get when he wasn't being manipulated into the "correct behaviors" but was just being challenged to be as aware as possible. The atmosphere in the car was comfortable and without strain on the relationship.

In sports, the critical variables are often physical variables, whereas in work they may be physical and/or mental. The magic of Self 2 focus is not so dependent on which variable you select as it is on the fact that you are focusing on *some* variable. Focus on *any* variable can help put you in a state of nonjudgmental awareness and thus provide reduction of self-interference. So don't be overly worried about picking the "right variable." There are many that will work.

Focus on Critical Variables While Selling—Buying and selling are two of the oldest and most universal work activities. All of us buy and most of us sell. If not for a living, we sell our ideas, our labor, our points of view, our opinions. The general goal of selling is to "heighten the perceived value" of something to create a desired result. There are numerous books and courses on this activity that vary greatly in their approach. Yet it is very interesting to realize how much skill a person can develop simply by focusing attention when in the act of selling.

When addressing this subject in my seminars, I ask people how many have firsthand experience of five-year-olds. "How good are five-year-olds at selling?" I ask. The response is universal admiration for their skill at selling parents on what they want. "Do they develop rapport with the buyer?" Yes, quite naturally. "Do they handle objections creatively?" Yes, they certainly do. "Do they know the buyer's 'hot buttons'?" Intimately. "Do they ever fail to ask for the close?" Never. "If turned down by one decision maker, do they approach an alternate decision maker?" Invariably. "Do they use the same sales approach with each buyer?" No, they customize. "Does fear of rejection or fear of failure keep them from coming back and trying again?" No. Not until we've sufficiently conditioned them. "So what course in selling did these five-year-olds take to develop such mastery? Are they following some model of successful selling?" Or do they just interfere less with their Self 2 potential?

How did they learn these selling skills? I don't believe it was so much by watching their parents' selling behaviors, as by paying close attention to their parents' buying behaviors. Children are naturally enrolled in the course called "learning from experience." They have spent five-plus years in this school and they see no better way to learn than by observation, trial, error, and adaptation.

Children don't consider learning to sell as "work." It is just part of the natural process of learning to get what one wants. Clear about her goals and in touch with her desire, a five-year-old girl instinctively pays close attention to critical variables and adjusts behavior according to nature's law: what feels good and what works. Learning takes place from every selling situation. Changes in approach are made as one goes, as different ploys prove effective or ineffective with the individual buyer. The child develops all this skill without the help of abstract reasoning. As adults, when we combine our capacity for reflection with our innate ability to learn from experience, we have a most formidable asset.

What do we learn from this five-year-old about how to focus while selling? What are some of the variables that are within the awareness of the young salesperson? The first variable is her own motivation. She has a very clear concept of the desired outcomes and a lot of self-confidence and hope. But most important is the amazing sensitivity to the customer. She must be able to pick up subtle changes in interest level, subtle shifts in tones of voice that indicate the seriousness or lack of seriousness of a particular objection. She is also alert to where there are openings in the willingness of the buyer and where the doors are closed. These are obvious variables in selling, but are often missed by the more complex and "knowledgeable" adults. Sometimes it is by being more childlike and natural that Self 2 says things that produce better results than we ever would have anticipated. One such time occurred when I was asked to "sell" a group of salesperson trainers at AT&T on the Inner Game approach to selling.

Self 2 Focus in Selling at AT&T—As AT&T was preparing to become a competitive, market-driven company, it put a great deal of time and resources into building a sales training school for account executives in Boulder, Colorado. It hired the best consultants it could find and designed a state-of-the-art facility with the best available technical equipment and sales curriculum. Archie McGill, the vice president of business marketing, had decided that this was where the Inner Game could have the greatest impact in his organization. He had asked me to collaborate with a leading sales training company based in California to design an Inner Game training program for AT&T's account executives.

Bill, the president of the sales training company, and I were invited to present our program at AT&T headquarters. It was my first time to make such a formal presentation, and as we were ushered into the very polished boardroom, I felt a little intimidated. I felt pressure from Bill to "get the sale" and pressure from everyone else to make this meeting worth their valuable time. The agenda called for the AT&T design team to make the first presentation. They took an hour to make a very well organized and thoughtful presentation with elaborate slides. Their primary training point was that account executives would sell "solutions to problems," not products. Learning to "uncover the needs" of the customer was thus a primary skill to be developed. Their vision, planning, and delivery were very impressive—as polished as the boardroom table—and to me just as intimidating. Finally, with a gesture of triumph, the slide presentation came to an end, and there were general nods of approval for a job well done.

Eyes turned to me. "Now we would like to hear your comments on what we've done and how the Inner Game might help us." I knew I could make the prepared presentation, but I could not see what it would contribute, since their presentation had covered all the bases. I sat for several moments thinking about what to do and I realized that there had been no real expression of any need on their part. Finally, I said, "I really don't feel very motivated to say anything," and stayed seated. The others were somewhat surprised; Bill was alarmed. He elbowed me forcefully in the ribs to encourage me to make the planned presentation.

Not venturing to the podium, I stood at my place and said with all sincerity, "I am very impressed by all you have presented.

From what you have told me so far, there are no problems and not much room for improvement. You have my congratulations for a job well done." I sat down.

Abruptly, the mood of the lead presenter, a former marine colonel, changed. His eyes moistened with embarrassment. In the next five minutes, he dropped his defenses and disclosed the considerable problems they were having. Hearing the expression of their need, I felt ready to present, much to the relief of my partner, who later asked me where I had "learned that ploy."

It hadn't been a ploy, and I'd never done it before. It was just Self 2 being honest. I hadn't calculated the results, but at the same time, I knew what I was doing. Fortunately, at the time, I didn't fully appreciate how rare such actions were in those corporate circles.

Perhaps the most important thing I learned about the Inner Game of selling was about trust. When buyer and seller trusted each other's integrity, the process was quite simple and could be done in a straightforward fashion without manipulation. Yet in most sales conversations I witnessed, there was a significant background of mistrust, not so much of the individuals involved as of the common practices.

Trust is definitely a critical variable in selling—perhaps the most critical. I have seen many sales training courses that instruct the salesperson on how to create trust. Most are manipulative in nature or become manipulative when they are used as techniques to accomplish an end. Usually customers learn over time how to resist the manipulations and the entire sales process suffers.

Trust is like sincerity—it is difficult to define and impossible to "manufacture." The easiest way to create trust is simply to avoid doing those things that undermine trust and to be quick to repair breakdowns when they occur. Trusting the customer to buy what makes sense requires letting go of manipulative techniques. As a result, a different kind of conversation opens up, one in which the salesperson becomes more focused on the important elements of the customer's *buying* process.

An Exercise: Focus on Interest Level—In an exercise designed for AT&T account executives, two volunteers were asked to role-play in the buying and selling of a used car. They were given five minutes to conduct the sales conversation. The salesperson was instructed to simply focus attention on the changes in interest level of the buyer over the course of the five minutes. He was told not to try to do anything to influence the interest level, but just to observe it. Similarly, the buyer himself and the students watching the exercise were asked to observe the buyer's interest level and record their observations at the end of each minute on a simple graph.

At the end of the exercise, the salesperson and the buyer were asked to graph their observations. The buyer's graph looked like this: 3 4 7 5 7.

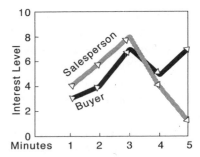

The salesperson's graph was 4 6 8 4 1.

The salesperson was asked what he observed. "The interest level was building pretty steadily until the end. Then I gave up and totally lost him."

The buyer was asked the same question. "Well, I was interested until I felt an objection during the fourth minute. Something changed about the salesperson. He seemed to get much more relaxed and comfortable, and I was ready to buy right away."

This was a shock and a big learning experience for the salesperson. At the moment he gave up, the customer had become ready to buy! And he hadn't seen it.

"I thought I had done a lousy job in answering the last objection," said the salesperson, "so I let go."

"I suddenly felt the pressure to buy was gone, and I was surprised at how it changed my readiness," said the customer.

What the salesperson learned was that, without knowing it, he was putting pressure on the buyer to buy and unwittingly causing resistance to buying. When he let go of the pressure, the resistance subsided. He had, in fact, prided himself on his persistence and had been critical of himself for giving up at the end.

Focus on the customer's interest level reduced Self 1's interference and heightened Self 2's learning and creativity. Salespeople also discovered that the quality of their listening could have a great impact on the buyer's communication. People know when they are being given full attention. They also know when you are just waiting for them to finish so that you can make your point. When one person gives full attention to another, it tends to become contagious, affecting the quality of both participants' speaking and listening.

Focusing on Results—In an Inner Game seminar for managers, a successful dentist asked how the Inner Game focus on critical variables could be applied to doing a better job managing his office. The problem was simple: Patients were spending too much time in the waiting room. His standard was that no patient should have to wait more than twenty minutes. He had tried many traditional management techniques to remedy the situation, but nothing had worked.

There were many different variables that could have been used as a focus to provide the learning that would bring improved results. I suggested focusing on the desired results themselves. "Since time is the final critical variable here, why not focus on how long patients *are* waiting in the waiting room," I suggested. Since most of the office staff were not in a position to observe the waiting room, they could only make informed guesses by observing variables within the range of their direct observation. It was to be a simple awareness game in which each employee would write down at the end of the day his best estimate of the number of patients that had been kept waiting more than twenty minutes. The goal was to make the most accurate estimate possible, rather than to improve the performance. The next morning, all their guesses were posted as well as the correct number based on the direct observation of the receptionist. I suggested the dentist run the experiment for two weeks before taking recommendations from the team about what, if any, changes should be made.

The dentist called me two weeks later, very excited and very surprised. At the end of the first day, there had been a drop from a previous average of fifteen people kept waiting to ten. At the end of the fifth day, there were none. The entire second week averaged less than one person a day kept waiting. He had asked his staff what they were doing differently and no one could say. "So it worked," he said, "but I don't know why."

I didn't know why either, but I wasn't surprised. What I did know was that people became more aware of critical variables and, without knowing exactly how, started making better use of time. I also guessed that because no one felt that they were being "managed" into getting better results, there was less resistance from the staff to the exercise. The formula of heightened awareness and reduced interference was again producing positive results.

Time as a Critical Variable—Time is a critical variable of most work activities. Probably the most common complaint of people who work, at every level in an organization, is "I don't have enough time to get done all that has to be done." The amount of time one has to complete a given task can be seen as either an aid to focus or its enemy.

An executive friend of mine made a very illuminating and succinct statement about time management. "No one can ever succeed in managing time. If anything, time manages you." As I thought about it, I saw that "time management" was a total misnomer. Time was something our Self 1's might like to think they can control, but in reality, "ol' man river just keeps on rolling along" and we can't do anything about it. At best, we can make intelligent choices about what we do within time. But time itself is out of reach of our managerial abilities.

But what we can do is become more aware of time in relationship to the tasks before us. Many people make lists of what they want to accomplish in a given day and are then surprised by not getting done what they thought they would. Could it be that we aren't aware of how long certain tasks take us?

A Time Awareness Exercise—A basic premise of the Inner Game is: Before you go about trying to change something, increase your awareness of the way it is. If I wanted to learn how to make better use of my time, I could make an estimate of the time I expected it would take me to accomplish each task on my to-do list. Then before actually looking at my clock to check how long a particular task took, I could make a guess. Then I could check the time it actually took. (This exercise might require jotting down the duration of unexpected interruptions.) I just might be surprised. I think most people would find that they are not particularly aware of the passing of time, even for routine tasks, much less tasks that they have less experience with. As we practice becoming more aware of time in relation to task, we are bound to learn some very interesting and important lessons that will improve time-task effectiveness.

Promising More Time Than You Have—There was a period of time a few years ago that I was feeling particularly overwhelmed by my workload. I couldn't understand why I seemed to be behind on so many projects. I decided to take a few minutes to write down all the projects I had committed myself to and to estimate the total amount of time it would take for me to fulfill each of my commitments to each project. When I added up the total of all the time I had committed, I realized that even working at highly effective levels of performance, I had committed about 200 percent of my available time!

When I had agreed to take on the projects, the decision was

based on my thinking that they were worthwhile, in terms of profitability, importance, my interest in them, or a combination of all three. When saying yes to each project, I felt good about it, even noble. But, like everyone else, I had a limited amount of time—twenty-four hours per day. I had promised time that I did not have. If my time were money in a bank, it was as though I had $240 and I had promised $100 to three people and then another $40 to five more people. It just wasn't possible. It also wasn't honest.

My Self 1 can be arrogant enough to think that it can undertake whatever projects it wants without considering the limitation of time. Self 2, though boundless in its potential, aims for the greatest economy of action and effort in keeping with purpose. But even so, Self 2 cannot do the impossible, particularly when Self 1 adds to the problem by interfering with focusing on any of the tasks at hand.

Noticing What You Notice—In any situation, one of the best ways of finding a critical variable to focus on is to notice what you are already noticing. What does this mean? If you ask three people to look out the same window and then ask each one to tell you what "stood out," they will come up with three different answers. Of the thousands of possibilities in the entire scene, one person notices that there's a hole in the roof of the farmhouse in the distance, another the colors of the sky, another the turning leaves on a nearby sycamore tree. The same thing takes place when you meet a person, or view a business problem, or look at a product. Everyone's attention is selective. What is being selected can often tell you something important about the viewer, as well as about what is being viewed. When coaching either an athlete or a businessperson, listening for what stands out in a given situation gives valuable clues about where to direct the focus of attention.

For example, a team of managers I was working with asked me to help with improving the quality of their meetings. When I asked the standard question, "What stands out for you as you observe your meetings?" three simple observations were made: (1) "We don't stick to the agenda." (2) "Meetings neither start nor end on time." (3) "A few of the people do most of the talking." It would have been possible to do an in-depth analysis of the meetings and generate from them a set of remedies to change behaviors. The approach I took was simpler. I asked one manager to focus on "adherence to agenda." He would do no more than raise his hand each time he observed the conversation wandering. Another manager observed the starting and ending time of the meeting, an observation that evolved into tracking the amount of time allotted and spent on each agenda item. A third manager kept track of the frequency and total length of time each person spoke. No corrections were ever recommended or enforced. But over the next few weeks, merely by virtue of the team's heightened awareness of these variables, meetings started and ended on time, there were fewer and fewer instances of wandering off the agenda, and participation became more evenly distributed and speaking more succinct.

I used to tell tennis students that if they didn't like the instructions coming from a tennis professional or a partner, they could always change the instructions from a behavioral command to the observation of a critical variable. If the pro said, "You aren't hitting the ball in front of you," they could simply start observing where they were in fact making contact with the ball, trusting Self 2 to make the corrections automatically. In the same way, many requests for change from a manager, from a customer, or even from yourself are often best handled neither by compliance nor resistance, but by simple observation of the variables embedded in the "command." In a performance review, a manager might be told, "You have to stop being so critical of your subordinates. I've been getting a lot of feedback from them about you on that." Perhaps the manager agrees. But instead of internalizing the command "Don't be critical," what would happen if he simply decided to make "criticalness" a variable to observe, in his own communication and others'? If he decided just to take notice and see what happened? I'm guessing that after he actually became aware of how much of it was happening, he would then find it decreasing—or at least becoming more appropriate.

Selecting a Critical Variable—There are three elements to keep in mind when choosing a variable to focus on. First, it should be *observable*. One of the functions of focus is to keep your attention in the here and now. It follows that the object of focus should be directly observable in the present. For this reason, the body language of the person you are communicating with would be a better variable than "gaining agreement." Second, it helps if the variable is *interesting*. Listening for the subtleties of feeling and intention in any communication is more interesting than just tracking the content of what is being said. As was demonstrated by the AT&T operators, there is a great deal more to listen for in a voice than information alone. Third, an effective critical variable is *relevant* to the goal of the task at hand. Among all those that are relevant, there may be one or more that require your attention the most—either because you tend to ignore that particular variable or just because it is particularly crucial. For example, a salesperson who is learning to apply less "pressure" might want to focus on signs of openness or resistance on the part of the customer. Such an awareness exercise would contribute to the task at hand as well as to the desired learning.

There are obviously many variables that Self 2 will track when focused. Below are some important variables in effective selling and buying mentioned by various salespeople in training courses. I offer them not as an exhaustive set of variables, but just as an example of how any variables can be used.

Trust—noticing your own and the other person's candor and openness.

Respect—looking down, looking up, or looking straight across as equals.

Control—who is controlling the flow of the conversation? When?

Time—time spent speaking versus time spent listening.

Clarity—of perceived need, of perceived value. Obstacles?

Pressure—on either side versus respect for choice.

Motivation—level, direction, timing, on both sides.

In general, I have found it best to select a critical variable that is simple and easy to observe: "bounce-hit" in tennis; speed of the car while driving; interest level in selling. A variable should not be intellectually demanding. Rather it is a neutral place to focus your conscious attention that will allow the fuller use of Self 2 faculties. What is always surprising to me as a coach is to see that Self 2 is capable of very subtle and complex learning when the conscious mind is focused on something rather simple.

The efficacy of focusing attention is then twofold. First, it allows for a better stream of information to the brain—I see the ball better, hear the person better, and can therefore respond better. But the second function is that it reduces self-interference and allows greater access to Self 2. From this point of view it matters relatively little what the particular focus of attention is; as long as you are focused, there will be less obstructing your capabilities to learn and perform.

Outer and Inner Variables—Outer variables in any given task might include its stated purpose, the resources and tools available, other people, costs, time lines, and standards required. Inner variables might include motivation, attitude, values, assumptions, beliefs, definitions, context, point of view, and feelings. Both inner and outer variables are critical to success. Most people are more familiar with focusing on external variables, yet there is much to be gained by becoming more aware of the internal variables, as they are ultimately more within our control. Which variable you focus on is a matter of choice according to your performance and learning goals at the time.

Attending to Attitude—One caution. The more "internal" your focus becomes, the more important it is to be nonjudgmental. To notice an outer mistake may be less worrisome than to notice you have a "bad" attitude. It also takes a lot more courage to fix an attitude than an error. Once you are aware of what your attitude is, the maxim "Awareness itself is curative" holds true. Listening to Self 1 say to you, like a parent, "You have a bad attitude," is not awareness. It is just listening to a self-condemnation. It takes an effort to reach back to that part of your being that controls attitude. But when you can get there, it is possible to bring thoughts and feelings into alignment.

Someone who was coaching me once explained that our thoughts and feelings can be like baggage in the overhead compartments of an airplane. If the attitude of the aircraft is too steep either downward or upward, the baggage will end up flying all over the compartment. No matter what you do to try to stuff it all back in place, you will fail. The only remedy is to find the control lever that changes the attitude of the aircraft.

Summary—There is no general skill more important to learning and the achievement of excellence than focus of attention. Like most skills, focus requires practice and conscious effort. Unlike most skills, though, it can be practiced during any and every activity—mental or physical. It also requires an offense and a defense. The offense involves making conscious choice about the critical variables, inner or outer, that need attention. The defense involves awareness of what distracts our attention. The practice of focus strengthens the muscles of attention and it also reveals, sometimes painfully, what still has the power to distract us. Focus then requires strengthening the muscles of conscious choice (Self 2) while weakening the pulls from our unconscious choices (Self 1). The next chapter looks at the unconscious attitudes we carry to work and offers a redefinition of work designed to make it easier to sustain Self 2 focus for longer periods of time.

Chart of Possible Outer and Inner Critical Variables

Task	Desired Outcome(s)	Outer Critical Variables	Inner Critical Variables
Driving a car	Get safely from A to B	Speed, space, position, road, weather, and car conditions	Attitude, focus, distractions, comfort level of driver and passengers
Communicating	Give and/or receive a message, come to agreement	The other person's interest level, clarity, conciseness, tone, relevance	Attitude, focus, what you are listening for, your level of respect, feeling, point of view, assumptions
Physical Work	Accomplishment of task, learning, enjoyment	Time, your body, tools, economy of movement, the task itself, other people	Attitude, focus, ease, balance, stress, boredom, enjoyment, purpose
Mental Work:		Time, vision, information, specifications, resources, alternatives, consequences, and the other people involved	Attitude, mental safety, point of view, assumptions, desire, doubt, criteria for evaluation, purpose
Problem Solving	Solving the problem, learning, enjoyment		
Planning	Creating the plan		

5

REDEFINING WORK

Does Your Definition of "Work" Make a Difference?

Just as "playing in the zone" is possible in sports, so working in a state of Self 2 focus (or the "flow state") is possible at work. But there are several steps to take before this state can be sustained for more than short periods of time. What I discovered in sports was that a person could maintain Self 2 focus as long as the coach was there to "hold" the context of nonjudgmental awareness and trust. While some players were also able to spontaneously re-create the same space for short periods of time on their own, something would always come up that would interfere with the magic. Self 1 would regain control, the player's default modes would reemerge, and it would be back to performance as usual.

Learning to focus and to refocus again and again is the first aid in decreasing self-interference. But sometimes first aid is not enough: surgery is necessary. To sustain focus for longer periods of time requires looking more deeply into the "meaning" or "definition" given to the activity at hand—whether it is tennis, golf, music, relationships, or work. Our definitions become the contexts in which we do these activities and thus exert great influence on our thoughts, feelings, attitudes, and actions. Because they are usually derived from the background cultural conversation, they are often invisible to us. But if they can be seen, they can be changed. A simple change of context can present an entirely new range of possibilities and, at the same time, exclude an entire range of interferences.

At work, we carry with us definitions of *boss, customer, product, employee, the company, ownership, goal* and *fairness*. Some of these are objective realities, but we all carry subjective interpretations of the words. In many ways, these definitions determine what we see as "reality" and thus how we respond to that perceived reality.

What Definition of "Work" Do You Bring to Work with You?

Most people define work almost exclusively in terms of the external results produced by the work. Building a house is work. Loading a truck is work. Selling a car is work. Running a corporation is work. Work is about *doing,* and tends to be defined solely in terms of the results. Here are some of the most common answers I get when I ask people what words they associate with "work":

- What I must do versus what I want to do.
- What I do for pay.
- Getting "the job" done.
- Doing what the boss tells me to do.
- What I do that's associated with "hard," "challenging."
- Accomplishment.
- Obligation, duty.
- Responsibility, accountability.

Our definitions are mental constructs, like internal lenses through which we view reality. Sometimes we can only guess at what they are through a process of deduction. Sometimes they become known in moments of direct insight.

This chapter is dedicated to examining the definition of

"work" that we carry with us when we go to work. We are used to thinking of definitions as meanings of words found in dictionaries. We are not so used to thinking that we have a choice in the definitions we accept and that those definitions can make a difference. But the meaning we give to "work" becomes the context and the background conversation for all our actions at work. Let's look at an example from the world of golf, where the impact of context is more readily visible.

What will the average golfer say if you ask the question "Is golf a pressure-filled game?" When I ask, the answer is usually "Yes, definitely." But then I ask the golfer how he would explain where this pressure comes from to someone who doesn't know anything about the game except the rules—to a Martian, for example. The Martian says, "I understand golf is a game where you hit a ball until it goes into a hole and you count the number of hits to get the ball into eighteen different holes. Where is the pressure?"

The golfer explains that hitting the ball into the hole isn't as easy as it seems. The Martian says, "I understand that, but the rules of golf say if you don't get the ball in the hole, you simply put a higher number on your scorecard."

"Exactly," the golfer says. "That's not a good thing. You might lose your bet to the people you are competing with."

Martian: Do you lose more than you spend to play this game in the first place?

Golfer: No, not usually. But another thing that happens is that your handicap goes up.

Martian: And then what happens?

Golfer: It's a matter of pride and self-esteem. If you score poorly, especially when you are capable of better, your self-esteem tends to be affected.

Martian: Oh, I didn't read about that in the rules of golf!

Golfer: Well, it isn't written; it's just understood by us golfers.

At this point in the discussion, the source of the fear and pressure experienced by the golfer is evident. It comes from a definition of the game that puts self-esteem on the line. The Martian, not having participated in the background cultural conversation that gave rise to such a definition, saw only the physical difficulties of the game. He would not have experienced the same fear and pressure if he had played.

Likewise, if the golfer could recognize that his definition of golf was merely a definition, an assignment of meaning to the game that he had accepted from the culture, he would be in a position to change his definition. He could play a different "game" while playing golf and in doing so avoid the seeds of fear that were latent in his former definition.

So is there another way to define work? My own effort in redefining work has been to create a definition more in keeping with Self 2's inherent nature and capacities.

Redefining Work: An Exercise

There is a simple process for redefining any important word. Start by asking where you got your current definition. Then you can evaluate that definition and make any changes. I like to create a three-column chart for this exercise (see pages 83–84). In the first column, I put down memories that contribute to my current definition of the word. In the second column, I put the definition that came from that source. In the third column, I assess the validity of my old definition in light of my current purpose and values. It is important to see that there is no correct "objective" definition of work. What influences our experience of work is the definition that we have formed subjectively. Making a conscious choice about the lens through which we experience work is what redefinition is all about.

What's the Benefit in Making a Change to the Old Definition of Work?

When I look over my work redefinition chart, I see the recurrence of the inner demand to enjoy, learn, and express capabilities through work. I also see the tendency to feel pressure from the outer demands made on me by other people and by society. There are two competing agendas running throughout my work life: my own inherent agenda, often unrecognized, and the agenda everyone else has for me. The latter does not go unrecognized. Its demands are spoken in no uncertain terms by the different people in my life and in an unspoken way by society itself. When I was growing up, the voice of "the others" seemed very big and powerful. Sometimes it had my best interests in mind; sometimes it had its own interests in mind. Resistance seemed possible only in token measure. Integrity with my self became increasingly difficult as childhood faded and training and indoctrination, in my case to "become someone," began in earnest.

I doubt it would have been possible to say to the world, at a young age, "I am here—so I already *am* someone. Let me alone." I believed that "they" knew what life was about and the way it should be lived. I also knew that I did not know. I was dependent on what my parents and society told me.

So a Self 1, which embodied these voices, emerged within me. It looked for approval and direction from those it was dependent upon for safety and acceptance. Whether I was alone or with people, Self 1 was always there, a judgmental audience ready to make its criticisms or grant its approval. The goal was to become someone worthy of respect in the eyes of this audience.

Meanwhile, Self 2 was relegated to a background position. Though less obvious, and unfortunately less heeded by me, its nature was still to find joy in self-discovery and expression. It took whatever opportunities were given it to live, love, and learn. It was not until I was in my thirties that I came to recognize and again honor Self 2.

The Cornerstones of My New Definition of Work

When my Self 2 was most present, there were an ease and excellence in *performance,* a self-generated interest in *learning,* and a natural *enjoyment* independent of the results of my work. These elements existed simultaneously and were mutually supportive.

Memories of Work	Contribution to Definition of Work	Current Assessment
CHILDHOOD WORK (5–13)		
· Helping Mom bake cookies and Dad wash the car.	· Work is doing something fun with the people you love.	· A good start.
· Chores: sweeping patio, making beds, washing cars alone.	· Work is assigned and done before play. Regular basis. Tied to allowance.	· As work becomes a requirement with external rewards and consequences used as motivators, joy diminishes.
· Daily homework assigned at school. Contests conducted and grades given.	· Work is measured. Grades are used to measure achievement and aptitude. Work becomes a competitive activity.	· Introduction to work as competition opens door to various forms of self-interference. Intrinsic motivation and joy diminish.
HIGH SCHOOL AND COLLEGE WORK		
· Schoolwork done under serious pressure to get into a "good college."	· Work associated with demanding time lines, stress, difficulty.	· Sense of one's own agenda replaced by the agenda of succeeding in the system.
· Summer job picking apples. Paid by basket.	· Physical work tiring but less stressful. Work = money = independence.	· Direct relation between effort and monetary reward creates strong performance momentum.
· In college decide to split time into working for grades and working to learn. Long-term assignments. Pressure of preparing to "earn a living."	· Survival and success depend on grades. Working for grades different from working to understand.	· Conflict between individual's and system's agenda leaves little room for enjoyment of work.

Memories of Work	Contribution to Definition of Work	Current Assessment
U.S. NAVAL OFFICER		
· Being a line officer on a guided missile cruiser in charge of people who know more than me.	· Work is being assigned an area of responsibility and getting work done through others: Command and control.	· "Command and control" environment pushed by fear and pulled by power. Much of Self 2 potential lost to the individual and the organization.
DIRECTOR OF ADMISSIONS AT A MIDWESTERN COLLEGE		
· Designing and producing an idealistic educational enterprise	· Work is creating something from nothing. Compensation is a by-product.	· Work that provides meaning is a motivator. Possible to let "the cause" supersede the needs of self.
PIVOTAL YEARS 1969–1971		
· Sabbatical club tennis pro in California. Reinvent teaching of tennis.	· Work is learning from experience while helping people.	· What is learned while working can be of greater value than the pay and more enjoyable than play.
· Become a student of "inner" possibilities of being human	· The possibility of work as an expression of gratitude.	· The opportunity to work as an expression of one's love is rewarding.
THE INNER GAME OF WORKING		
· Coaching, writing books, lecturing, seminar design and delivery, corporate seminars, conducting a business.	· The possibility of work as a meaningful contribution to others while bringing enjoyment, learning, and financial compensation.	· The choice to accept work as an opportunity for making a meaningful contribution while receiving in return learning, satisfaction, and financial compensation.
· Volunteer work.	· Work for the joy of participating in a valued purpose.	· The intrinsic benefits of work can absolve the need for financial gain.

They became the cornerstones of my new definition of work because they were aligned with Self 2, whose agenda I had decided to learn to listen to.

In my old definition, work was performance alone. In simplest terms, *work* equaled *doing*. But connected with that definition were all the Self 1 judgmental meanings attributed to doing something *well:* success, failure, competence, incompetence, being better than one person, being less good than another.

But learning and enjoyment are still inherent dimensions of work, even if we're not paying attention to them. You are either growing, evolving, and developing your capabilities or you are stagnating. In the worst-case scenario, you are "devolving" while working—becoming less yourself. Regardless of where you happen to be on the spectrum, the learning component is part of working.

The same is true with *enjoyment*. You are feeling *something* between agony and ecstasy while you are working. Even if we numb ourselves to the point of "not feeling anything," it's almost impossible to avoid wanting to feel better. The need to enjoy is universal. What varies is the degree to which we acknowledge and value this component of our lives. Too often we believe that enjoyment is what has to be sacrificed to the goal of excellence. The best performers in all fields provide much evidence to the contrary. Most of us also know from personal experience that we perform better when we are enjoying ourselves.

The Work Triangle—In my seminars, I draw a triangle with the words *performance, learning,* and *enjoyment* at the points. "Do these three components of work belong in a triangle? Are they interdependent?" I ask.

The answer is usually yes, they are interdependent. Then I ask, "If the learning side of the triangle were increased, would it affect performance and enjoyment?" Obviously yes. "Likewise, if enjoyment were greatly decreased, would it have a negative impact on both learning and performance results?" Again, yes.

PERFORMANCE

LEARNING   ENJOYMENT

"Which of these three aspects of work are most emphasized by the culture in which you work?" I ask. This question is met with general laughter, as if too obvious to be asked. "How much more is performance emphasized than learning and enjoyment?" I place my pen in the center of the triangle and begin to move it slowly up toward the performance apex of the triangle.

"Tell me when to stop." When I am nearly at the apex, a few say, "Stop there." There is usually a chorus of objections from the rest saying, "No, keep on going!" They won't let me stop until the pen is well outside the boundaries of the triangle.

It is obvious to most people that emphasizing performance doesn't make it happen. Quite the contrary is true. The three sides of the work triangle are part of an interdependent system. When either the learning or the enjoyment side is ignored, performance will suffer in the long run. When it does, management feels threat-

PERFORMANCE

LEARNING   ENJOYMENT

ened and pushes even harder for performance. Learning and enjoyment diminish even further. A cycle ensues that prevents performance from ever reaching its potential.

Learning While Working: An Idea Whose Time Has Come—The time
has come to acknowledge learning as a real component of work and not merely a chance by-product. I doubt that anyone reading this book has not been told in a thousand different ways, "We are living in a world of accelerating change. . . . We live in the information age. . . . The amount of information available is doubling every few years. . . . As fast as we learn new information and technologies, they become obsolete. . . . This is the era of the Knowledge Worker."

Peter Drucker, author of *Post-Capitalist Society* and more than twenty other books, is one of the most influential thinkers about the history of modern management, its current state, and its future. He coined the term *knowledge worker* in reference to the fact that knowledge in the head of the worker, more than any other resource, makes the world economy move. Says Drucker,

> *Knowledge is different from all other resources. It makes itself constantly obsolete, so that today's advanced knowledge is tomorrow's ignorance. And the knowledge that matters is subject to rapid and abrupt shifts—from pharmacology to genetics in the health care industry, for example, or from PCs to the Internet in the computer industry. The productivity of knowledge and knowledge workers will not be the only competitive factor in the world economy. It is, however, likely to become the decisive factor.**

The most obvious implication of the "knowledge worker" is that work is inextricably linked with one's ability to learn. For the knowledge worker, merely "getting the job done" is a waste of time unless "know-how" has been increased in the process. The old

---

* Peter Drucker, *Post-Capitalist Society* (New York: HarperBusiness, 1994).

definition of work said you took what you already knew and used it to produce results for profit. The new definition says that work is a process of growing your capabilities while in the process of producing results in order to be better able to produce future results.

In the knowledge age, learning as well as performance contributes to bottom-line profit for the individual worker and the enterprise, as well as to the economic health of the society. In the recent industrial economy, it may have been true that a company could succeed by hiring people with the know-how to perform certain functions. This is becoming less and less true. Only those companies that have developed the capability to *grow capability* are going to succeed.

Enrolling in the Greatest Seminar on Earth—If learning is so critical to success, where and when is it going to take place? The demands of modern work allow few hours and limited dollars for training. I want to recommend a seminar that takes very little extra time and no extra money. It is, in my opinion, the best seminar ever designed. It's not mine, but I'm a student in it and it is the source of my most valuable knowledge, skill, and personal development. It is highly interactive and has incredible 3-D graphics. Best of all, it is perfectly designed to teach me exactly what I most need to learn.

This seminar is your everyday life. You've been enrolled in it since you were born. The part of this seminar that is about *work* is going on every minute of every working hour. The quality of this seminar should not be taken for granted. To design an artificial seminar of such magnitude and complexity would be a daunting and unimaginably expensive undertaking. Think of what would go into designing all the props and events, the infinite variations of consequences resulting from your individual choices, to say nothing of the valuable interactions with all the other participants in the seminar. What I like most about this seminar is that it is "mass customized." A hundred people in the same situation can have a hundred different learning experiences, perfectly tailored to their own individual needs.

And what is the price of admission into this seminar? The humility and interest to be a student. You must declare yourself to be a *learner* during your working hours as well as a doer. After that, you must pay *attention* to the teacher—experience itself. Once we pay those dues, the ball will teach us how to play tennis, the customer will teach us how to sell, the subordinate will teach us how to manage, the followers will teach us how to lead, and every work project will teach us how to optimize our work.

This *seminar of experience* has an open-door policy. You can enter and exit when you choose. When you enter and pay attention as a student, the learning process begins. You start from your present understanding and move at your own pace. But if you get so involved in the drama and the trauma of your work that you forget you are a student, the seminar goes on without you. It waits patiently for your return, always granting the freedom to be conscious or unconscious, to pay attention or not. And the variety of courses to enroll in is nearly unlimited.

There are many reasons to engage in this seminar. The desire to learn is as fundamental to our being as the desire to survive and to enjoy. We are changed by the way in which we work. We develop qualities as well as skills. Intellectual, emotional, creative, and intuitive capacities are developed through our work experiences. Determination, courage, commitment, empathy, imagination, and a host of communication skills are built. We may not *see* this learning happen if we focus only on performance, but in retrospect we can tell that it has occurred.

Distinguishing Learning from Performance Goals—Most people who work are used to setting and pursuing performance goals. Once you enroll in the seminar of your daily work experience, it becomes important to make a distinction between a performance goal and a learning goal. Most workers will give you a blank stare if you ask what their learning goals are, or they will offer up a performance goal in disguise. For example, "I would like to learn to make more money" and "I would like to learn to break eighty in golf" are simply performance goals with the word *learning* inserted.

How does a learning goal differ from a performance goal? Performance is something you *do* that brings about an observable change in the external world. Learning, on the other hand, is a change that takes place within the learner, although often as a result of interaction with the external world. Thus a change in understanding based on new information or on a new interpretation of old information would be classified as learning. Likewise, the added know-how to be a more capable communicator, problem solver, airplane pilot, or leader would all be changes that take place within the individual and are therefore achievements in learning. Take a look at the lists below.

Performance Goals
1. Increase salary by ten percent before the end of next year
2. Build a more effective team
3. Increase shareholder value
4. Get a better job
5. Finish my report for my boss
6. Create a personal development plan

Learning Goals
1. Double my reading speed
2. Increase my understanding of market dynamics
3. Overcome fear of rejection
4. Eliminate stress
5. Enhance my listening skills
6. Develop empathy

The performance goals may or may not require any change in capability on the part of the performer. They each describe a single external accomplishment. The learning goals, on the other hand, represent changes in capability. Though their achievement may have little value in itself until the new capabilities are applied in the world of performance, each learning goal has the potential to contribute to the attainment of countless future performance goals. The difference in leverage gained between the development of a capability and the accomplishment of a specific task is largely underrated in a performance-oriented culture. The building of a bridge is a wonderful achievement, but gaining the competence to build a bridge could lead to the construction of many bridges.

Precisely because learning takes place *within* the individual, it is not easy to observe until you see the results of the learning showing up in the world of performance. Learning cannot be measured in the same way as can performance. And the strategies and tactics that may be suitable for attaining performance goals may not apply to learning. This is one of the major reasons why many individual and organizational learning initiatives fail.

Remember that learning is about the unknown. Learning goals can be set only according to what you already know about what you want to learn. But much of what you will learn is material that you didn't know you didn't know. How are you going to set goals about that? Try to be as clear *as possible* about what you want to learn and why. Then be prepared to follow your interest and be open to the unexpected.

The next questions to ask yourself are: *Where* will this learning take place? What parts of my work experience are best suited to teach me what I want to learn? It may be your conversations with clients or co-workers, or your planning process, or a specific task or project. What will be your method of learning? What questions or critical variables might you use to focus on your work experience?

Example: The Salesperson as Learner—Let's take the example of a salesperson who has been out in the field for two weeks selling his product and now joins his sales manager and colleagues for a regular sales meeting. Normally, what questions can you expect from the sales manager? They will generally focus on *performance:* the number of customers called upon, the number of sales closed, revenues compared to goals, recognition for good performance, criticism for poor performance. Strategy, tactics, and plans will be revisited, and perhaps the manager will offer some "inspiration" to motivate maximum effort during the next period of selling.

What if the manager asked what was learned about the customers' needs or perspectives, what the competition is up to, or new ways of handling objections? There are countless questions that *could* be asked to gather and share the *learning* that occurred. If only one salesperson had been in the learning mode while selling, there would be interesting answers to these questions—answers that in fact might have come from conversations with customers who *didn't* buy. And these answers might have contributed learning to the individual, the sales team, and the company that would result in greater future revenues.

A focus on learning also sends the message that there is "gold in the hills" in addition to the sales themselves. A good salesperson delivers learning as well as sales. The irony is that if focus on performance eclipses the learning, performance itself will suffer.

The salesperson as learner not only brings home the sales, but realizes that what might be learned about customer need, how to uncover it, how to elicit unspoken objections, how to deal with customer concerns, fears, and resistances, and how to look at the situation from the customer's point of view, are all integral and fascinating parts of selling. Such a salesperson becomes a student of the art of selling while performing the functions of selling. In one case, he may make a sale but learn nothing. With the next customer, he may fail to make the sale but learn a great deal that will benefit him and his company. Once he realizes this, the game of selling is changed for him forever.

Let's say Anne realizes that she has difficulty coping with customers who bring up lack of financial resources as an obstacle to buying her product. In the performance context, whenever this concern was expressed, she would either get defensive and back down, or get overly aggressive and cause the customer to back down. As a student of her work experience, she sets a learning goal to find more creative responses. Specifically she decides to find tactful questions that present the customer with realistic consequences of buying or not buying. Simply by setting this learning goal, she has changed the way she will respond to her next customer. Instead of fearing the moment when the customer brings up costs, she now welcomes it as the only way to fulfill her learning goal. As a result, she is not defensive or aggressive. There is a space in her brain for generating questions that are helpful to the customer and for coming up with creative solutions to their financial problems.

Anne has discovered a means of coping with a troubling situation and has taken real steps to resolve her fear of rejection. As a result, she has benefited greatly from the very customer situations that used to frighten her. What she has learned will benefit her personally and professionally. She is in a position now to share something of value with her co-workers and to learn from their experiences. Acknowledging the benefits of learning inspires more of the same. In this way, learning can become contagious and spread organically through the people in a team or organization.

Of course, the best salespeople realize this without being told. But most often they aren't asked to share their learning with the team. "Just give us the numbers. . . . Thank you very much." The learning conversation just doesn't happen in the team and would probably be considered "strange" because it doesn't fit into the established definition of work. As a result, individual salespeople may fail to recognize its importance to themselves, the team, the customer, and the company.

On the other hand, I've worked with companies whose sales force embraced learning and enjoyment as well as performance in their definition of their work, and who met with amazing success in all three dimensions. Salespeople were encouraged to set specific learning goals as well as performance goals and were asked to share what they learned with the entire team. Good questions were valued as much as good answers. Customers were looked at as "teachers," not just potential buyers. A lot was learned about building lasting relationships with customers—not from "tricks," but by learning from each and every interaction with the customer.

Setting Learning Goals: QUEST—In thinking about possible learning goals, there is one word that I find particularly useful. It's a word that comes from one of the most basic activities of the learner—to question. The word is *quest*. Whereas a question can merely reflect idle curiosity, a quest is something one pursues in earnest. It implies a great sense of commitment. One may entertain millions of questions but pursue only a few quests.

Besides being a word that inspires the learner, *quest* is also an acronym for five different kinds of learning goals, each of which expands one's capabilities in a different way.

> **Q**ualities
> **U**nderstanding
> **E**xpertise
> **S**trategic Thinking
> **T**ime

Qualities—When managers are asked what qualities they most want their team members to bring to a given project, they may generate a list that includes responsibility, integrity, initiative, creativity, task orientation, persistence, clarity, cooperation, etc. Each of us has all of these qualities and more within us as potentialities. But we have learned to bring out some of them more than others. Which qualities would you like to see more of in yourself? Which would others on your team like to see more of, or less of? Learning to access and express any chosen quality or attribute is one kind of learning goal that anyone can set for himself or herself.

Understanding—Understanding requires more than just information. It requires comprehension of all the components of a particular subject or system and the relationships among the components. You can have a great deal of information about a job without really understanding it. I may be able to state the mission of the company or of a given project, but do I understand that mission sufficiently to be effective? Ask yourself this question to establish a meaningful learning quest: Given my current performance goals, what, if understood better, would make success easier or more likely? Such goals might be stated in terms of "Expand my understanding of . . ." (for example, my co-workers, my boss, the customers, the competition, market dynamics, systems and processes, finance, obstacles, etc.).

Expertise—Expertise is what I call know-how or skill. It can be technical or nontechnical. Ask yourself: What skills could I hone or develop that would enable me to attain a higher level of performance? What skills am I learning that I could apply to my present or future job? Which of these skills can be learned from experience on the job and which need some book or classroom learning? What skills are already developed and don't require more time and attention? You could choose to develop certain computer literacy skills, negotiating skills, communication skills, accounting skills, technical skills, management or leadership skills, or master a given body of knowledge. The enhanced expertise, once developed, becomes available for use in a wide variety of future tasks.

Strategic Thinking—Strategic thinking can be viewed as a quality, a skill, or an understanding. But it is a distinct kind of thinking. It is the ability to step back from the trees and see the forest. It is the ability to lift one's thinking above short-term goals and view long-range objectives. It is a critical component of work capability—not just for a few leaders, but for everyone in an organization. Ask yourself: How strategically am I thinking? Do I have a strategic perspective, or merely a tactical one? How clear are my priorities at work? Are my current activities in line with my long-term objectives? Am I thinking independently enough? Is my work life balanced and in harmony with the rest of my life? Is my definition of work my own? Do I see my job in relation to the other jobs being done around me? Do I see what it has to do with the overall mission of the team or company? Do I think strategically about my whole life? Setting such a learning goal means not only setting strategic goals in some area of your work or life, but also developing the habit and ability of strategic thinking to be used wherever and whenever needed.

Time—All work is done in time and is related to time. Learning this relationship is critical to successful work. The best strategies and the best experts have failed because of an inability to come to terms with this fact. Does your work get done on time? How aware are you of the time required for completion of the tasks on your to-do list? Are you feeling constantly pressured by time? Are you constantly behind your time lines? Do you procrastinate? If so, you might consider setting for yourself a learning goal around the relationship between time, task, and priorities. (See "A Time Awareness Exercise," page 71.)

A Process for Learning from Experience—The Inner Game approach to learning is based on the fact that the most valuable learning and development will take place from your interaction with your work experience. The most common excuse given for not pursuing learning at work is "I just don't have the time." But the beauty of learning from experience is that it is done simultaneously with the work and therefore requires very little *extra* time. A little time is needed for what I call a "learning brief" to set one's learning goal prior to a given work experience. Then, after the work experience, a short time for reflection, what I call the "debrief conversation," takes place. Both conversations can be done alone or with a coach and need take only a couple of minutes each.

During the learning brief you can get clear on what you want to learn and where to focus attention. The most important purpose of the brief is to remind you to be a learner during the given work experience. The debrief conversation can be used to reflect on what you observed during the work experience and to allow for insights, new questions, and possible next steps to emerge. These quite naturally become a part of your learning brief for the next work experience.

The Experience Sandwich

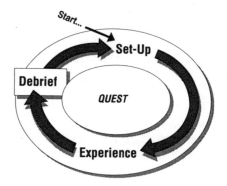

The period of work experience between the brief and the debrief can vary from a short task to a long-term project. What is important is that you are engaged in the learning process while working, and moving toward learning objectives that can be used in future work and, when appropriate, shared with co-workers. Using this process to learn more from experience is a very practical application for whatever you find valuable in this book. Because we feel so time pressured, engaging in this process takes a little discipline. But workers who have developed a habit based on this process report that the time taken for the learning brief and debrief conversations amounts to a very small fraction of the time saved by virtue of what they learn.

The following are examples of learning brief and debrief worksheets used in Inner Game of Work seminars.

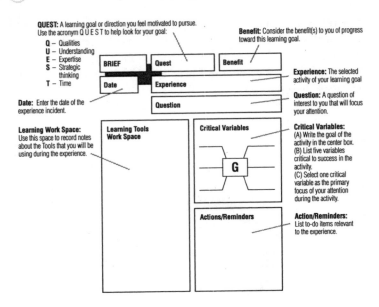

QUEST: A learning goal or direction you feel motivated to pursue.
Use the acronym Q U E S T to help look for your goal:

  Q – Qualities
  U – Understanding
  E – Expertise
  S – Strategic thinking
  T – Time

Benefit: Consider the benefit(s) to you of progress toward this learning goal.

Experience: The selected activity of your learning goal

Question: A question of interest to you that will focus your attention.

Date: Enter the date of the experience incident.

Learning Work Space: Use this space to record notes about the Tools that you will be using during the experience.

Critical Variables:
(A) Write the goal of the activity in the center box.
(B) List five variables critical to success in the activity.
(C) Select one critical variable as the primary focus of your attention during the activity.

Action/Reminders: List to-do items relevant to the experience.

BRIEF · Quest · Benefit · Date · Experience · Question · Learning Tools Work Space · Critical Variables · G · Actions/Reminders

Enjoyment as a Component of the Work Triangle—The quality of a worker's experience is probably the least-acknowledged *result* of work. The common belief is that if it's work, it's not supposed to be enjoyable. No pain, no gain. In some cases, people assume that if you do not feel "stressed out" or "burdened," you aren't working *hard* enough or are probably not "pulling your weight." Then there is the adage "Find a job that you really enjoy, and you will never have to work another day of your life." The assumption is that if you are enjoying what you are doing, it is not work.

There is a long-standing Puritan tradition behind this attitude, and behind that a long-standing feudal tradition of workers being motivated by fear. The Puritan ethic was rooted in the idea that worldly success and future salvation were linked. Being successful was understood as a sign of grace and an indication that one was among the few chosen for salvation. Success was a result of embracing good Puritan values of hard work, thrift, and self-discipline. Emphasis was on the hardness of work and certainly not on any joy possible in the act of working. The feudal tradition embodied the notion that workers could be *owned* by landlords. In exchange for work, landlords allowed workers the means of survival. Both traditions contributed background definitions of work for the industrial age. But this is all being challenged by the postindustrial world and by changes in the beliefs and values of people who work.

The belief that people should enjoy their work—either by finding the kind of work they like or by finding ways to like the work they have—is gaining ground in most developed countries. At the same time, the notion that the worker is merely a means of production *owned* by an employer is in retreat. With it is going the notion that workers owe their work lives to a single employer. Command and control as the primary means of decision making is being replaced by systems that allow greater participation in decisions by everyone affected by those decisions. Workers are realizing that their capabilities and knowledge control the eventual success of their companies. Most workers in developed countries

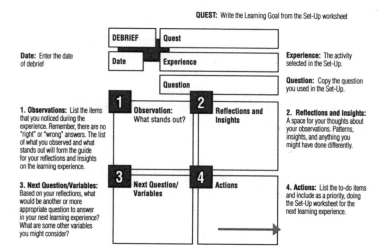

QUEST: Write the Learning Goal from the Set-Up worksheet

DEBRIEF | **Quest**

Date: Enter the date of debrief

Date | **Experience**

Experience: The activity selected in the Set-Up.

Question

Question: Copy the question you used in the Set-Up.

1. Observations: List the items that you noticed during the experience. Remember, there are no "right" or "wrong" answers. The list of what you observed and what stands out will form the guide for your reflections and insights on the learning experience.

1 **Observation:** What stands out?

2 **Reflections and Insights**

2. Reflections and Insights: A space for your thoughts about your observations. Patterns, insights, and anything you might have done differently.

3. Next Question/Variables: Based on your reflections, what would be another or more appropriate question to answer in your next learning experience? What are some other variables you might consider?

3 **Next Question/Variables**

4 **Actions**

4. Actions: List the to-do items and include as a priority, doing the Set-Up worksheet for the next learning experience.

are in a position to fulfill needs and desires at work that go beyond the necessities of survival.

That there is a growing measure of freedom for the individual worker does not mean that each is truly free. Observing thousands of people walking into various corporate headquarters on Monday mornings, I cannot say that what I see on their faces are expressions of joy. Many still look as though they are being dragged to work by ropes. Yet there are others who walk with a determination that says, "I've got something very important to do, and I'm on my way." They may look a little grim, but they are motivated. Then there are a few who don't look as though they're going to "work." They seem happy to be alive and doing what they are doing. I appreciate this kind of satisfaction when I see it in others and when I feel it in myself. For lack of a better term, I will simply call this experience the state of *enjoyment*. And this is the state in which I would like to spend as many of my working hours as possible.

The Goal of Enjoyment at Work—How to approach such a goal? Enjoyment seems to come more as a gift than as a consequence. At the same time, I have observed the many ways in which I and others interfere with the possibility of enjoying ourselves while working. One way to approach the goal of enjoyment at work is to get rid of as much of that interference as possible. Another approach is the realization that enjoyment is inherently preferable to misery. The child does not have to be taught how to enjoy. It comes naturally. Perhaps we have been taught how *not* to enjoy, and therefore we have to unlearn it. This is a fascinating challenge.

Let's start by recognizing that we really have no choice about feeling something while working. How we *feel* when working is an inescapable part of working, no matter how hard we might try to ignore it. We are somewhere between misery and ecstasy while working. The questions that matter are: Where are we on that continuum, in which direction are we moving, and does it really matter to us?

I invite you to complete the following self-assessment. It involves rating your work life on a one-to-ten scale, where ten equals the most enjoyment you have ever had while working and one the least. (Note: If you don't relate to the word *enjoyment,* use whatever represents the way you like to feel while working.)

State of Being While Working	Percent of Your Work Time Spent in This State
Enjoyment (8–10)	
In Between (4–7)	
Misery (1–3)	

The next step is to ask yourself two questions: (1) "What contributes to my enjoyment while working?" (2) "What contributes to my misery while working?" Here is a small sampling of answers to these questions given by people taking Inner Game of Work seminars.

On what contributes to enjoyment:
"When my heart is in it."
"When I'm doing something for someone I want to please."
"When I'm getting along with my co-workers."
"When the entire team is working together for a common purpose."
"When I know that what I am doing is making a valued contribution."
"When I am acting out of choice, not pressure."
"When I like the work I am doing."

On what contributes to misery:
"When I am in conflict with co-workers."
"When my workload is beyond my capabilities."
"When there is insufficient time to do a quality job."

"When asked to make changes for no apparent reason."

"When the work is routine and there is nothing to be learned."

"When I feel everything I do is being evaluated by myself and/or others."

"When I feel disrespected by myself and/or others."

"When I lose control of direction and am just putting out fires."

"When I've overcommitted my time."

"When I'm too emotionally attached to the results."

"When I'm not trusted."

As I look at this list, I see one underlying critical variable to enjoyment at work: The worker's relationship with himself. To the extent I value myself, my time, and my life, I will not allow myself to work in a state of stress or misery. Enjoyment of every moment becomes an important priority wherever I am. I have to ignore the indoctrination that told me this was selfish. Experience has shown me time and again that it was only when I was enjoying myself that I did my best work and could make my best contribution to others.

The first step toward improving the quality of one's enjoyment at work is to simply become more aware of it as it is. I have asked golfers, a group notorious for their commitment to performance results, to keep score of their level of enjoyment while playing. At each hole, they mark the number of strokes taken and a score of one to five for their level of enjoyment. At first, there tends to be a strict inverse relationship between the number of strokes and the level of enjoyment. They enjoy it more when they play well, they've explained matter-of-factly. However, as they become more aware of enjoyment as something worth having on its own, they realize it is possible to obtain whether they're playing well or not. Without any effort on their part, golfers find that the time they indulge in misery after a poor shot decreases, and that the enjoyment of the walk or ride between shots increases.

The same is true at work. Many times we try to ignore how

we feel while working. We ignore it because we don't see how it contributes to excellence and we may not think it's important. The chart on page 101 can be used as a daily practice of awareness of enjoyment. The critical variable is to be aware of how you are honestly feeling during any segment of your work experience. Then, whenever you want, you can reflect on what contributed to the enjoyment or lack thereof. Give simple awareness a chance before rushing in and trying to "fix" the situation. You might be surprised to find the extent to which awareness itself is curative.

A Sales Team That Decided to Make Enjoyment a Priority—One sales manager I know believed so strongly in the value of balancing the work triangle that he took what I considered a rather extreme measure. His team had the worst results of any team in the company for the previous six months. He had done everything in his power to try to improve performance results and he constantly talked about increasing revenues. But he figured that he had little to lose in trying to rebalance the triangle. He announced that for the following quarter, he was suspending all sales quotas! He let the sales team know they were to continue selling, but that they would not be held accountable for reaching any specified levels of revenues. What he expected them to do was to learn how to have fun selling. He asked his salespeople to rate their current enjoyment levels on a scale of one to ten and to set any goals they wanted to improve their "enjoyment" scores.

During subsequent sales meetings, they discussed what they had done to bring more enjoyment to their work as salespeople. Most became much more aware of what interfered with their enjoyment. For some, it was fear of failure. For others, it was following rote procedures. Others discovered that they were working themselves to the point of exhaustion. Performance results were not even discussed, just submitted on short reports.

To the great surprise of the sales team as well as their manager, by the end of the quarter, the team was leading all others in the company in sales results! When they reviewed the experience of their best quarter ever, they were amazed at what they found. On the whole, their team had spent 25 percent less time with customers, yet had seen the same number of total customers. They had spent 30 percent less time planning their presentations and 30 percent less time on paperwork. But the conclusion was that the real benefit had come from the quality of the relationship with the customer. They were more relaxed with the customer and vice versa. Customers seemed to be more open about their problems and needs and more responsive to the team members' recommendations. Each salesperson knew that he was getting more sales, but thought it was a fluke until he found that the total revenues of the team had increased by 40 percent for the quarter.

None of the specific elements of this example should be taken as a prescription. But the general notion that quality of enjoyment is linked with quality of learning, which in turn is linked with levels of performance, is worth pondering.

Increasing enjoyment at work is not always easy. Many things happen that are frustrating. Many things aren't in our control. Problems come in an unending stream. People we relied upon can let us down. Worst of all, we can let ourselves and others down. Money can be lost. The market can tumble. We can be laid off. We can make mistakes. Our bosses can be creeps. Our team leaders can be incompetent. Bureaucracy can get in the way of our effectiveness. The list of things that can prevent us from enjoying our work is endless and, for the most part, inevitable.

Yet there are those who enjoy working. The key is that they enjoy *themselves* while working. They make a distinction between themselves and the results of their work. This distinction brings a detachment that allows for enjoyment independent of circumstances. Maintaining this distinction takes conscious effort, but it is worth it. The alternative is that your enjoyment will always be dependent on whether or not things happen to be going your way.

Finding Your Balance in the Work Triangle

The relationship between performance, learning, and enjoyment should not be static. It's like riding a bicycle. You have to do more than pedal. You have to steer as well. You have to keep your balance. And you can't really be told how to do all this. Furthermore, there is no way to define the correct proportion of the variables for riding a bike, just as there is no "correct" proportion for the three elements for work. The key is maintaining a dynamic but balanced relationship, allowing yourself and the work situation to determine the emphasis.

Self 2 naturally shifts and balances priorities according to the situation. If you are going on vacation, enjoyment takes the lead, yet hopefully some learning will occur, and you have to pay enough attention to performance that the packing gets done and travel arrangements are made. If you are reading a book, taking a course, or pausing for reflection, learning will naturally take the lead, but hopefully there is some enjoyment in the process and performance goals are being appropriately served.

Throughout any workday, the priorities shift naturally with the situation. There are critical moments in any work situation that call for emphasis on performance. Perhaps little else in those moments is important. But after that critical situation has passed, it is time to stop the performance momentum in order to reflect and to learn. The important thing is to find and maintain a balance that works for you.

How Is the Return on Investment of Your Work Time?—Looking at work from the point of view of Self 2 can bring a new perspective to the work experience. When the value of your work is measured solely in terms of what you get for your performance, you can easily feel shortchanged. The amount you earn for your labors, after taxes and bills, may not equal what you think your time is worth. It is easy to feel ripped off or exploited. But before you decide to seek alternate work, make sure you have evaluated the total ROI (return on investment) of your work time.

The work triangle shows that from Self 2's perspective, the compensation package for work comes in *three* forms. Besides the compensations for performance itself, it includes the benefits from learning as well as the rewards of enjoyment. I give my effort and

I give my time, a limited and most precious resource. I bring with me the potential I inherited at birth and have developed since. If my capabilities grow, I have even more to give tomorrow, and thus potentially more to earn. I am getting paid to produce, but if I am learning while working, I am increasing my economic potential. I have been paid, not just by the employer, but by Self 2, by the level of enjoyment I am earning.

Every day I have given some of myself and have collected these three forms of payment. What I want to make sure is that the balance is positive. Is it possible to give more than you get? It is possible and in fact very common for a worker to be on the losing end of his return on work. But beware that it's not your own Self 1 ripping you off. You can always quit a job that you don't like and try to find another. But that won't necessarily get rid of your over-controlling Self 1 boss. The only way I know to do that is to allow more and more Self 2 in and be willing to give up some of the Self 1 demands for approval, recognition, and ego gratification.

Self 2, on the other hand, gives where there is good return. Take the example of Mother Teresa, who received very little material compensation for a great deal of hard work. When told by one visitor, "I wouldn't do this for all the money in the world," Mother Teresa reportedly nodded and said, "Neither would I."

We don't have to be saints to shift the balance of payments from Self 1 to Self 2. It just takes a commitment to oneself. I want to learn, I want to enjoy, and I want to be productive. I want to remember why I am working and whom I am really working for. When a few individuals make the commitment to their own learning and enjoyment, they serve as catalysts for others by the qualities they express while doing their work. Those who accept such a challenge may accomplish much more as a result of their work than the performance results they are compensated for.

6

FROM CONFORMITY TO MOBILITY

The pursuit of working free is not the pursuit of freedom from responsibility or from the demands of bosses, companies, or customers. It is about choosing to work in a way that is truly responsible to yourself—a way that is in sync with your own choices, values, and concerns. A redefinition of work, being only a mental model, cannot in itself make this possibility real.

The patterns of Self 1 conditioning that conceal the aspirations of Self 2 are strong and permeate most work environments. Norms and definitions have been formed over many years and they limit the possibilities we can see for ourselves. The pressures to conform to external norms and models—to do and think as we have done and thought in the past—distract from our internal compasses and thus from thinking independently. We live and work in groups and we find it difficult not to think like the group.

There is an ancient tension between the living "fire" within an individual and the "forms" forced on him by the society in which he lives. *Conformity* is the word I use when the individual gives priority to the external form over the internal fire. Finding satisfaction at work becomes increasingly improbable as an individual or culture allows conformity to quench our inherent fire.

Conformity can be attractive and it has its own compensations. It offers a kind of safety based on the appearance of being, doing, and thinking like others. It offers convenient ways to blend in socially. In superficial matters, conformity may cause no harm. But when one bases life decisions on external voices at the expense of listening to one's inner self, something of the greatest value can be lost.

Many who know the cost of conformity rebel against it to protect their integrity as individuals. But rebelling *against* something has never provided the kind of freedom that satisfies. For that, one must learn to listen to the promptings of one's deepest and most authentic self. I have learned to welcome the urging of Self 2 as it pushes through the rigidities of my borrowed thinking. It is this urge that shows me I'm still alive and kicking, even if I'm not yet totally free. When I recognize and honor this urge, it becomes stronger and stronger. It is the harbinger of someday flying free.

The conflict between the massive forces of society and the inherent needs of the individual hardly seems to be a fair contest. On the one hand, we have a faint impulse from within asking that we heed it. On the other hand, we have the pervasive models of conformity surrounding us, suggesting that we adapt ourselves to them. Hundreds of magazines show us how we should look and dress. On TV and in movies, we are offered countless models for how to think and behave. Norms are set and norms are followed without thinking whether they are in our best interests. Those who can't or won't follow the accepted norms are made to believe they are wrong. They are treated as failures, in need of correction. Those who follow the norms and succeed become our heroes and model setters. There's so much external pressure and such a small voice within. Outside seems so big and inside seems so small.

But inside has one big advantage—it is *always* there. Wherever you go, Self 2 will speak to you if only you learn how to listen. Another advantage is that Self 2 is biased toward enjoyment. We like feeling good. And we are biased toward living together harmoniously. Because of this inherent bias, we respond to the beauty of a sunset, enjoy the taste of good food, like to love and respect others, want freedom and integrity, and have an urge to understand what is important to us. Having DNA on your side is no small advantage in this contest between the fire and the form. But it is still a formidable contest and it takes considerable courage as well as wisdom to win.

Redefining work as performance, learning, and enjoyment in keeping with Self 2's innate desires is a giant step toward working free. The next step is to attempt to understand why conformity is so attractive to us and how it affects our ability to work free. The word I find most helpful in discussing this concept is *mobility*. It connotes not a specific destination but the ability to move in any desired direction without self-constraint. Mobility is the quest for movement driven by the free human response to one's own deepest inner urgings. Keeping this possibility in mind, let us take a brief look at the alternative—a sense of being and action in conformity to external pressures, rewards, and punishments.

An Initial Attempt to Break the Bonds of Conformity

Until I was in college, I saw little alternative to conformity. The prevailing norms and definitions of success were so pervasive, they were invisible to me. It wasn't until my second year at Harvard that I took a course that woke me up and helped me realize that I was more a product of my conditioning than I thought. The occasion for this minibreakthrough occurred during a course called Natural Science 114: The Science of Human Behavior, offered by Professor B. F. Skinner, then on his way to being proclaimed the father of behaviorism.

I had chosen the class out of an interest in learning more about myself and how human beings "worked." On the first day of class, after scanning the audience for some time, Professor Skinner said, "I am a little alarmed that there are not more Radcliffe students in the audience. . . ." As he paused, I wondered what he could possibly have meant. "This course is going to give you Harvard guys an unfair advantage over them." According to Professor Skinner, this "unfair advantage" was not merely an educational one, but an "advantage" in getting our way in the age-old "battle of the sexes." He certainly had my attention as he went on to explain that the class was about learning how to understand and control human behavior. Professor Skinner seemed to be saying this not just to motivate his students, but to express his utter belief in his methods and his serious concern about giving undue advantage to the men.

There were only two texts to read for the class, both written by Skinner: *The Science of Human Behavior* and *Walden Two*. The first presented the theory that human behavior could be controlled by positive reinforcement of desired behaviors. The course description in the Harvard catalogue read, "Emphasis upon the practical prediction and control of behavior and upon the implications of a science of behavior in human affairs." The second was a novel based on a "utopian society" established on Skinner's principles of "human engineering." Skinner's theory was quite simple. Behavior of all animals, human animals included, is the result of responses to various negative and positive stimuli in the environment. Those behaviors that result in positive reinforcement tend to be repeated while those that result in negative reinforcement tend to be avoided. You can't really know scientifically what happens "inside" the subject's mind because you can't observe it, but you don't need to. All you need to do is to control the reinforcers and you can thereby control the resulting behaviors.

Professor Skinner demonstrated his methods in the laboratory with his famous "Skinner box," a cage wrapped in gauze, with a pigeon in it. He asked, "What do you want me to have the pigeon do?" Someone called out, "Have it jump in counterclockwise circles on its left foot." I thought it was an unfair request and would be impossible, but Skinner didn't flinch. He just got to work on controlling the pigeon's behavior—in the same way, as he would later explain, that the more complicated human being's behavior could be controlled.

The Skinner box was fitted with a food trough that would

make food available to the pigeon whenever Skinner clicked the appropriate button on his remote. His remote also controlled the light in the cage and the ringing of a bell. The pigeon, which I gathered was quite hungry at the time, was strutting around the cage exhibiting normal pigeon behaviors. Skinner was watching intently. The moment he saw the pigeon do a distinctly leftward movement, he would click the buttons on his remote, the light would go on, the bell would sound, and the food trough would open. The pigeon would peck at a little food before the trough was closed again. The bird then resumed random pigeon behavior until Skinner noticed another element of the desired end behavior. The process went on: light, bell, food, and an increasingly greater number of counterclockwise movements on the part of the pigeon.

After about half an hour, the pigeon was definitely favoring its left foot and turning more to the left than to the right. Still, I was thinking, at this rate of learning, there was no way the pigeon was going to be jumping in counterclockwise circles on its left foot by the end of the lab. It also occurred to me that there was a fair exchange going on between Skinner and the pigeon. "Is Skinner training the pigeon to jump, or is the pigeon training Skinner to feed it?" I wondered. But soon Professor Skinner made a small but significant change in his methodology that accelerated the process considerably.

He pushed the buttons that triggered the light and the bell, but not the food! Now Skinner didn't have to wait for the pigeon to go to the trough and eat. He explained, "At the beginning of the period, the light and bell were 'neutral' stimuli for the pigeon. They were neither negatively nor positively charged as reinforcers of behavior. They were neither rewards nor punishments. But after being *associated* with the food, the light and bell themselves became positively charged and could be used as positive reinforcers of behavior." This was the moment of truth about who was training whom. The pigeon received no actual nourishment for its efforts, making it clear to the observers who was really in control.

To me, the implications of the Skinner demonstration were

chilling. To what extent were my behaviors and my choices the re-sult of conditioning from my environment? Who or what had its hand on the remote? Whose agenda was I living? And if human behavior was conditioned by reinforcers that were merely *associ-ated* with real needs, then what were the "lights and bells" that had me jumping in "counterclockwise circles" at Harvard? Could my general sense of dissatisfaction at that age have come from the fact that I wasn't getting enough real food?

I thought about applause at the end of a victorious tennis match in a grandstand court. The applause was merely a sound, just like a bell, yet what would I do for that sound? Of course, the sound was associated with "recognition" and "approval," but was this real food or another association?

I thought of all the "jumping" I did in class to get an A. A lit-tle mark on a piece of paper—a mere symbol. Did it really mean anything? How important was it to me? What were others making of it and why? I was getting close to issues that I felt I "shouldn't" be questioning. If earning A's and winning tennis matches no longer seemed worthy of pursuit, my entire system of motivation and meaning would be vulnerable to breaking down. If society's definition of success wasn't any more than social conditioning to reinforce culturally desired behaviors, then what was real?

For a moment, I glimpsed the conformity that was surround-ing me. But I wasn't confident enough in myself at the time to put the conditioning aside. I could see no alternative to success as the system defined it. After all, I had gone to Harvard because I was told it was the best. "If I go to the best school and succeed there, I will be the best" was the logic of this pigeon. So I continued jumping and jumping until exhaustion took me to the verge of failure. And it was the prospect of utter failure that gave me the opportunity to glimpse an "exit" from my Ivy League "Skinner box."

Tiredness and procrastination had put me behind in my course work. Faced with the impossibility of catching up, I became so stressed that I had a hard time concentrating when I sat down to study. My eyes would pass over the page, but there was little or no focus. An exam was coming up in a political science course for which I had done almost none of the reading. I didn't think it was possible to get enough reading done to pass the exam, even if I had been functioning well. However, true to form, I decided to "pull myself up by my bootstraps" and give it an all-out effort. Three days before the exam, I took a full book bag of unread volumes to the library, saying that I would study the books for six hours straight whether or not I could concentrate well enough to understand their contents. The course I was studying for was called Government 180: Principles of International Politics; it was taught by a professor named Henry Kissinger.

I started by reading very slowly, word by word, and at the end of the first page, asked myself if I had understood anything. The answer was no. I could not recall anything I had read. Trying to read fast was no better. The stress I was feeling made it impossible to focus, and the more I realized that I wasn't comprehending, the more stress I felt. The more stress, the less concentration. A vicious cycle was happening. Regardless, I honored my decision and persisted for the full six hours. By the end of it, my eyes had passed over many pages, but, as far as I could tell, nothing had sunk in.

I collected my books, put them in my book bag, and walked down the stairs of the library toward the street. As I descended the stairs, a voice in my head said convincingly, "There's no way you can pass this exam." I accepted this statement as fact. As I was opening the door to exit Lamont Library, the voice said, in the same convincing tone, "If you can no longer read, you won't only flunk this exam, you will flunk out of Harvard." As the library door was swinging closed, I also accepted that statement as fact. At the instant the door clanged shut, it seemed that any possibility of success had closed behind me. As I stepped out onto Massachusetts Avenue, I had fully accepted that I had flunked out of Harvard. Though such a thought had never been imaginable to me, it was now an accepted fact.

The jig was up. I was out of college, and since that was my

only claim to success, I had flunked out of "success" itself. I, who until that time never allowed myself to flunk a single exam throughout my school years, had become, in an instant, a self-proclaimed total failure!

What happened next is difficult to relate. I was walking down Massachusetts Avenue as a failed student with nowhere to go. I could not think of going home and facing my family and friends, and I could not stay in college. I was at the end of one world without being able to see the next. Yet from somewhere deep within came the ability to accept this unimaginable fate. The only question that came to mind was simply "Now what?"

It was dusk, and on the street I saw a beggar whose legs had both been amputated at the thigh. He was sitting on a blanket on the sidewalk selling pencils. I had passed by him before and each time I would feel uncomfortable, caught in conflict about whether or not to buy a pencil. Now all such thoughts were gone. I looked at him and saw a fellow human being, no different from myself. I felt connected, equal in dignity, as one human being to another. I remember thinking, "I'm not looking up or down at this person—I'm looking straight across." It felt good to feel that I belonged to the human race.

Perhaps I had been looking for this feeling of connectedness for a long time—but had neglected it in my headlong pursuit of grades. I had associated A's with self-worth. Ironically, this taste of the "real food" I needed came when the external evidence of my worthiness had disappeared. I walked down the street, a new person. I looked at people differently. Instead of wanting to compare myself to them, I wanted to get to know them. With the door to "success" closed, stress was gone and I was simply glad to be alive, without any idea of what this life was about.

For a few hours, I lived life differently; I was out of my Skinner box, a free pigeon. A failed pigeon, but a greatly relieved one. Though nothing particularly eventful happened, I was looking out at life from a different perspective. Each moment seemed fresh and interesting. I felt no fear of talking with strangers and on subjects that hadn't previously interested me. I felt neither high nor low. I was neutral and very much in the present and was thinking clearly. I had been relieved of a terrible burden I had been carrying around without knowing it.

I awoke the next morning feeling very good and free of the normal stress. Then the same simple question occurred to me: "What now?" To continue going to classes was as good an option as any. But it seemed an option, not a must. Although I can't say I walked across Harvard Yard with an overwhelming enthusiasm to learn, the normal feeling of compulsion of "having to go to class" was gone. I was going to class freely. When I sat down and began listening to the same professors speaking about the same subjects, I was somewhat surprised that I was enjoying listening to them and found at least some of what they were saying interesting. What was gone was the constant internal assessments about whether I was understanding the material or would remember it during exams. I was even more surprised to find that when I sat down to read the book for Professor Kissinger's course on international politics, I got interested in the very text that I couldn't get through the day before. For the first time in weeks, I could read with comprehension and without worrying. And even though by final exam time the next day, I had done only half of the assigned reading, I did not feel stressed. I wrote essays based on what I knew and didn't sweat the rest.

By the following week, when my exam was returned with a C, I was confident again that I could function and get through my college work. Gradually, I returned to my normal academic study schedule and was able to focus, better than ever before. My grades were moving from B's to A's. As they did, I can't say that I didn't begin to lose some of that original sense of freedom. A's and the success they promised began to look good to me and, by imperceptible degrees, I soon found myself seduced again into jumping to the lights and the bells of the academic system.

I found that working free was not so easily maintained in that academic environment and that I hadn't quite made it "out of the box" for good. But I had felt the urge to be free and tasted the possibility of freedom and I would never entirely forget it. From that time on I knew the truth of the adage "We may need to live *in* a crowd, but we don't have to live like one."

I know that most people have felt this urge to be free even in the midst of adult responsibilities. It's not that we really want to be free *from* our responsibilities but to be free while acquitting our responsibilities. It's when our responsibilities are mostly driven by external pressures that we find ourselves dancing to the bells and lights of conformity and we lose touch with the urge to be free. As we do, it becomes harder to distinguish our real needs from merely symbolic ones.

What does it take to snap a person out of such a trance? Unfortunately, sometimes it takes a crisis or a tragedy. Sometimes it takes the failure of our dreams. Sometimes it takes exhaustion or illness. I look with admiration at Christopher Reeve, who says that he has known greater happiness as a quadriplegic, simply being alive, than he knew by being "Superman" to millions. What could those who are still trying to become supermen and superwomen in the eyes of others learn from his example?

If we could break out of the box of conditioned thinking, what would be left? What would be our true ambitions? What would be our own desire, and what dreams would that desire envision? How much would they differ from our present dreams? Where would we want to go and how would we want to get there?

To answer these questions, we first must delve deeper into the nature of Self 1 and Self 2.

Clarifying the Distinction
Between Self 1 and Self 2

How can the distinction between Self 1 and Self 2 be sharpened? I have called Self 1 an *invented* self or a mental construct, while Self 2 is the self we were born with, the *created* self. Since all of us were given the capacity to think, thinking is also a part of Self 2. But the concepts that we form by our thinking are separate and distinct from the self that conceives them.

These concepts, whether invented by ourselves or the result of external conditioning, influence us greatly. For example, if I identify with a concept such as "I am not good enough," I will probably start looking at my feelings and behaviors through the lens of that concept. I will also interpret how others view me through that same lens. And I will no doubt be able to find ample "evidence" to support my basic negative self-image. The negative concept is now fortified and will be used to find more supportive evidence. It is a self-fulfilling prophesy.

Realizing the power of negative self-concepts, some people try to reverse the process by affirming *positive* self-concepts. But the concept "I'm the greatest" is still merely a concept. Whereas a positive self-concept may produce more positive behaviors, I have never been satisfied with merely changing negative programming to positive. Although it is true that our thoughts about ourselves might be as reprogrammable as software in a computer, do I really want to see myself as a computer obeying its programming? For me, the important thing to acknowledge is that my self-concepts, whether negative or positive, accurate or inaccurate, are only mental constructs—they are only made of thought and they are not *me*. I am something else.

What I really am precedes any thoughts I may have about myself. It is this self that interests me, from its infancy through all stages of its natural development. When I acknowledge this self, I can give it credit for every quality, feeling, thought, urge, and behavior that is truly genuine and excellent. I have no trouble acknowledging the magnificence, kindness, and power of whatever created such beings. At those times, Self 1 doesn't hold much sway. I am content to be myself and have nothing to prove to myself or anyone else.

Of course, this self can be obstructed and distorted by my self-concepts, resulting in behaviors that are anything but genuine or excellent. When these distortions can be distinguished from Self 2, they can become part of the rich tapestry of our existence. It is then possible to find even more appreciation for the existence and qualities of Self 2.

There is no question that Self 2, in the process of its growth toward independence, is very vulnerable to a wide range of harmful and limiting misconceptions about ourselves. We all grow up in a community, whether large or small, and are easily influenced by the prevailing thinking of that community. Beliefs, values, and concepts are passed along to the new arrivals quite efficiently and quickly become part of our Self 1's "software." As we try to understand who we are and how we are viewed by others, our perceptions can be quite unstable and seemingly random. One day we see ourselves as accomplished, respected, and loved. Then, failing at a task or noticing that someone doesn't appreciate us, we shift to see ourselves as worthless beings, void of virtue or capability.

As our Self 2 evolves toward independence and increased awareness, it can learn to distinguish the conditioned software from its inherent nature and make choices about what to accept and what to reject. It is by exercising this capacity to make distinctions that we can rid ourselves of the distortions that inhibit our growth.

My passion for this subject comes in part from the fact that I have experienced some of the worst that Self 1 has to offer and have been fortunate enough to recognize and respect the best of Self 2. For me it is not the philosophical distinction between the two that is important, but the ability to *know* the difference. When I can connect with Self 2 through feeling, I can truly acknowledge it. I need to be aware of Self 2 within me. Then I can truly begin the process of self-discovery and the contrast with the merely conceptual self becomes stark. Although some combination of both selves will always be present in whatever I am doing, the point of the Inner Game is to learn to give full expression to Self 2 with a minimum of self-interference.

Finally, there is one aspect of Self 2 that did not have a great deal of emphasis in the Inner Game books on sports. It is the part of Self 2 that is capable of conscious and purposeful thought. While Self 2 was always given the credit for performance at our best, active thinking was not an important requirement for hitting a golf or tennis ball. In fact, in sports, performance seemed to be at its best when the thinking mind was still. But at work most of us need to think. Not only do we need to think about what we are doing, we need to think about *why*.

The capacity of Self 2 to be conscious—to create or recognize meaning, and to perform *purposeful* action is one of its most human attributes. Two people can be playing the same game of tennis but only one of them may know why. In the same way, two people can have the same job while only one of them is clear about the purpose of that job or why he or she should make an effort to do it well. The next segment of this chapter highlights the power of conscious thought and purposeful action at work.

EF—An Executive Friend

Over the past twenty years, I have engaged in ongoing conversations with many executives on the subject of optimal performance and developing people's capabilities in the workplace. Of all of these, there is one series of conversations that stands out as unique. The conversations were with a person I will simply refer to as "my executive friend." He is perhaps the most successful executive I know, not because of the position he holds, but because of his remarkable ability to execute his goals and dreams. In the course of many conversations with him, I learned a great deal regarding the growth and development of people at work. Over twenty-plus years, he has become a valued and most respected friend. Out of my respect for his privacy and the informal nature of our conversations, I will refer to him hereafter as EF.

Many of my conversations with EF took place while we played tennis. Without playing for points, we would hit balls back and forth, talking as we did so. Whenever the conversation required more focus, we would take a breather and finish the dialogue standing at the net. EF's declared motivation for playing tennis was the benefit of physical exercise, while mine was the extraordinary learning that took place from our interaction.

It is difficult to describe the impact these conversations have had on me. EF's remarks were full of common sense. They were simple and profound at the same time. Sometimes they were so simple that it was only out of my respect for his remarkable personal and professional success that I would take them to heart. I would go home after playing tennis and think about what he said. Sometimes it would be quite a while before I saw both philosophical and practical significance in what he said. EF does not consider himself a philosopher. As a practical man, he is interested in theoretical ideas insofar as they might help him accomplish his goals.

EF travels a great deal and his perspectives are drawn from a wide range of international experiences that encompass many cultures, yet seem to transcend them all. He is always more interested in what human beings have in common than in how they differ.

We spoke about the management styles of the West and the East, their mutual strengths and weaknesses, and about learning and communication within organizations. We spoke about the importance of individuals thinking for themselves and about how easily the integrity of the individual can be compromised by pressure from the agendas of the group or society that that individual is a part of. And in nearly all of our conversations, we discussed what it meant to succeed as a human being.

One day, after a particularly strenuous hour of tennis with relatively little talk, EF handed me a single sheet of paper he had printed from his PC, saying, "Here's a breakthrough in what we've been talking about. I'll be interested in what you think about it." I took the page home with great anticipation.

"Mobility"—The page had a one-word title: Mobility. It contained only a few hundred words of text with a simple graphic—a picture of the da Vinci universal man, legs and arms outstretched, with arrows indicating the capacity to move in all directions.

Like da Vinci, my executive friend is a genius in his field as well as a versatile learner in many others. Both give evidence of thinking that appreciates the appearances of things, but finds greater fascination with their deep underlying structures.

EF's text started with a simple introduction:

Here are some of the factors that can move people toward their desired goals or stop them from ever reaching them.

Next, there was a definition:

Mobility. The capability to move or be moved.

Then an elaboration on the definition:

Applied to us, it means the ability to move or adapt, change or be changed. It also means the ability to reach one's objectives in a fulfilling manner— to reach goals at the right time and in a way we feel good about. Therefore, mobility is not only change but fulfillment and harmony with one's progress.

Sitting at home, I wondered, "What did EF really mean by *mobility?*" At first, I took it simply to mean flexibility and timeliness in the accomplishment of one's goals. But "to reach desired objectives *in a fulfilling manner*" meant that both work objectives and personal objectives were to be met at the same time. This was a simple notion, but one with significant and profound implications. Clearly, EF saw that personal fulfillment was possible at work, but also understood that it was quite rare. The more common notion is that individual fulfillment is a consequence of the accomplishment of objectives. Mobility, in this new definition, means that both the destination and the journey can and should be fulfilling.

EF's next paragraph was about change and awareness. These

were subjects we had often discussed in relation to personal changes as well as to macro changes at the organizational level. EF was most interested in those insights that held true at all levels:

Moving in such a fashion brings about better awareness and the ability to make subtle changes when necessary. Being able to make changes within changes can make the difference between success and failure.

This is clearly what I had seen in the Inner Game process of coaching both sports and work. When the tennis player or worker became more aware of what was happening, inside and out, change would take place in an organic way. The process of learning in the awareness mode is subtle but effective. It is far less mechanistic and coercive than the command-and-control method. Harmony with Self 2 in the process of change allows for greater awareness, which in turn allows for the subtle changes to take place.

EF went on to describe one of the greatest difficulties faced by individuals and organizations in times of change—making changes for the sake of change:

When people feel certain frustrations, they tend to think that merely making changes will fix everything. But random changes produce random results.

If companies understood that last sentence, they would save billions of dollars and countless work hours that are wasted in inappropriate efforts to change. One of the things I learned in both sports and work was that I should *not* try to change everything that I thought should change. If the *needed* changes were attended to with nonjudgmental awareness, many of the other problems would correct themselves.

EF's next paragraph was difficult for me to grasp at first:

Changes are only of value when they are synchronized with all other elements and take place in correct proportion. Mobility gives us the ability to move, but not the reason. The ability to change does not guarantee that the changes made will lead toward success. Therefore, mobility must be closely tied to direction. Once one is removed from the other, both are rendered useless. Without direction, no successful change can take place.

I realized EF was talking about something akin to systems thinking. Nature is full of examples of systems that work only when all the necessary elements are present and functioning in sync with the other elements. If you make a change in one part of the system, you are liable to make an unintended change in another part and thus in the entire system. A chemical intended to clean a body of water may end up killing the algae that feed the fish that in turn help keep the water clean.

This phenomenon also exists in family systems, particularly those dealing with problems of addiction. When only the addicted family member receives treatment, the roles of the other family members who have been coping with the addiction are thrown out of balance. Sometimes there is so much disruption that it provides more pressure for the person to return to the addiction.

In business, there are countless examples of random changes that do not benefit the enterprise as a whole. A change designed to fix one problem causes ten others. Solutions in one department end up having a negative impact on another department, which finally comes back in the form of a much more serious problem.

To make specific changes that are in line with overall purpose and at the same time in sync with other changes being made requires an expanded level of awareness of all the important elements of a system. Initiating specific changes to solve specific problems without seeing their impact on the other components of the system can and usually does result in a short-term victory while contributing to failure of the system as a whole.

EF's page ended with a list of the five elements of mobility:

1. Grant yourself mobility, because you have it.
2. Have the clearest possible picture of where you want to go.

3. Be willing to make changes within your change.
4. Keep your purpose clear.
5. Keep your movement and direction synchronized.

That Is the Ultimate Mobility—The primary meaning I gathered from this page was that it was about attaining freedom of movement to fulfill internal and external goals. I also saw that it would require breaking the bonds to unnecessary external conformity and replacing them with a higher level of awareness and conscious thought. In some ways, this fit into what I had already come to understand about the importance of allowing Self 2 to have a greater chance to express itself. It was certainly in keeping with the work triangle and the need to meet learning and enjoyment goals as well as performance goals. It also valued awareness, choice, and trust. Mobility was the essence of what I had been learning about the Inner Game of working. Yet there was something more to this notion of mobility than I had yet understood, and I felt eager to learn.

How could I apply mobility to my own work life? Could I really find the process of working as fulfilling as the resulting achievements? What would it really mean to be satisfied with one's progress both internally and externally? Could I achieve mobility and then help my clients achieve it, too?

Taking the Steps—Let's take a closer look at what each of EF's instructions means in terms of your mobility and what you can do to remove obstacles.

1. **Grant Yourself Mobility, Because You Have It**—Think of an aspect of your work that you consider less than satisfying. Rate your satisfaction on a scale of one to ten (ten being the highest degree of satisfaction and one the lowest). Consider the three dimensions of mobility: (1) the contribution to the attainment of your external goals; (2) the contribution to your internal satisfaction; (3) how you feel about the amount of time given to this work to accomplish the above.

Let's say you rate your overall satisfaction as a 4–5, and let's assume you've been stuck at this level for some time. Mobility means that you can increase that level of satisfaction in all three dimensions. Mobility does not mean you know right now how to move from a 4–5 to an 8; it just means you acknowledge you can find out how to do it if you so choose.

Granting yourself this mobility so that you truly believe you can move toward greater work satisfaction is not always easy. Presumably, there are obstacles to your satisfaction or you would not be dissatisfied. But beneath all those obstacles, inner and outer, there lies a desire, a hope, and the ability to move toward your desired goals. To grant yourself mobility you may have to acknowledge *both* sides of the equation.

The inner conversation may be like this: "Yes, I believe I can move toward greater satisfaction in this aspect of my work, *but* . . ." It can help to acknowledge both the voice of optimism and the voice of doubt by writing them down. If the obstacles are in the forefront of your mind, then write them all down until you can't think of any more. Note which of these obstacles are external and which are internal. Then start acknowledging your inner resources. You have used these resources to get unstuck before. You have achieved certain goals before. And finally, remember that the essence of your ability to move toward your desired goals exists because *you* do—because you are a human being—and for no other reason. Acknowledging your inherent mobility can help you find your way around, through, and over your obstacles, both real and imagined. It is your first and most critical step.

The most common block to acknowledging mobility is thinking that your circumstances make mobility impossible. Granted, there are always some things that are beyond your control. But they can't stop your inherent mobility. Mobility is independent of circumstances. It is independent of the past. It is even independent of whether you think you have it or not. Mobility doesn't focus on what it can't control, but moves by making changes in what it *can* control. My own experience is that even in moments of great hopelessness, the mobility is still there waiting to be acknowledged in order to become activated.

The easiest way to convince yourself that you don't have mobility is to form ironclad concepts of yourself and how you do things: "This is the way I am and this is the way I do things." Freedom is about realizing that you always have the choice to start moving in any desired direction regardless of your past. This is the essence of the first step. You have mobility and always have had. You just may need to remind yourself of the fact from time to time.

There is a well-known quotation of Johann Wolfgang von Goethe, the eighteenth-century German poet, dramatist, novelist, and philosopher, that addresses the great power available to those who have the courage to grant themselves mobility. "Concerning all acts of initiative, there is one elementary truth the ignorance of which kills countless ideas and splendid plans: the moment one definitely commits oneself, then Providence moves too. All sorts of things occur to help one that would never otherwise have occurred. A whole stream of events issues from the decision, raising in one's favor all manner of unforeseen incidents and meetings and material assistance which no man could have dreamed would come his way. Whatever you can do or dream you can do, begin it. Boldness has genius, power and magic in it. Begin it now."

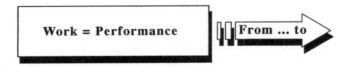

Work = Performance   From ... to

2. Have the Clearest Possible Picture of Where You Want to Go—Once you have acknowledged that you have the ability to move in any desired direction, the next step is to get the clearest possible picture of your desired destination. I believe EF picked the word "picture" intentionally, because in goal setting, pictures are definitely worth a thousand words.

It is more effective for a golfer to "see" the trajectory of his golf ball rising into an arc against the sky, then falling onto the green and rolling into the hole, than it is to say to himself, "I want to hole this shot." Likewise, if your goal is better teamwork with your colleagues, it contributes to mobility to envision what that might look and sound like. When you use pictures, sounds, and words to project a desired future state, more parts of the brain are involved in the goal setting. This increases the likelihood that more of your brain will be used in the process of fulfilling the goal.

I once did a goal-setting exercise with the senior managers of a large company in the midst of a major transition. Their written goals were vague and divergent. But when they were each given crayons and paper and asked to draw pictures of both their present situation and their future state, there was an astounding similarity in the resulting pictures. Six of the ten drawings contained an image of a brick wall that had been broken through. Until then, there had been little or no acknowledgement that major obstacles existed. Furthermore, there was common agreement about the nature of the obstacles represented by the brick walls. Thus, important information that already exists within us can sometimes be more easily accessed by images than by words.

It is commonly said about goal setting that all goals should be specific, measurable, and realistic. Though I have achieved many such goals, I do not like to limit the envisioning process to these criteria. My most important goals have started out rather vague, quite impossible to measure, and would have definitely seemed unrealistic at the time. I try to keep my promises specific and realistic, but aspirations should know no bounds. The important thing about goals is that they come from desire.

When, as a coach, I ask tennis players what they would like to improve in their game, they might say, "I would like to get more shots over the net and into the court." When I then ask how many more shots they would like to get in, they might say 50 percent or 70 percent. "Don't you really want all your shots to go in?" I reply.

The answer is always, "Yes, but I don't think that is a realistic expectation." This is true, it is not a realistic expectation, but it is a realistic *desire*. You don't hit a shot because you want to miss it. You want every shot to go in. You may also want each shot to be graceful and enjoyable. It's okay to keep expectations realistic, but desire is a different thing.

Desire wants what it wants. Desire is a *feeling* that can produce a picture or a vision of what it wants. It may or may not be similar to what other people want, but true desire is never borrowed from anyone else. So the hardest thing about getting a clear picture of your direction is to be able to distinguish *your* picture from that of the many pictures that are painted by other people.

Performance goals may be more easily measured than your learning or experience goals, but that doesn't make them more important. I am reminded of an interview with Michelle Kwan, the Olympic figure skater, after she had failed to win the gold medal in the 1996 Winter Olympics. She was asked by the reporter to describe how disappointed she had been. She said that her real goal had been to skate her best in the games. "And I believe I did," she said. "I skated my heart out, and I brought home the silver. And I feel very good about it." Clearly she had two goals—one to win the gold, the other to skate her heart out. One was specific and measurable, but I got the distinct feeling that the other was more important for her. I remember feeling proud that she didn't buckle to the pressure from the reporter to make her feel she had failed.

When it comes to setting goals, some people say, "You can have anything you set your mind to. You can have whatever you can imagine you can have." I am very cautious about statements like that. When I look back on my life and consider the events, the people, even the circumstances, that I value the most, very few of them are things that I could ever have imagined. I have a good imagination, but I don't want to settle for what can be imagined by me or anyone else. I want to live beyond the limits of my imagination as much as possible.

In getting a clear picture of one's desired destination, it is important to make a distinction between means and ends. Often people won't let themselves get in touch with what they truly want if they don't see the means of getting it. This is why some people find it impossible to figure out what they want. As soon as the desire emerges into consciousness, a doubt intrudes saying, "Forget it, there's no way." So most people forget it. But desire and means often arise independently. If I can have the courage to acknowledge my desire as it exists, without necessarily knowing how to fulfill it, mobility can start. Maybe all I can see is a first step toward a seemingly impossible goal. But when that step is taken, another step that I couldn't see before becomes apparent. And after a few more steps I may get an even clearer picture of where it is I really want to go. "Where there is a will, there is a way" is the mantra of people who have realized that they have mobility.

So before thinking about the means to the end, simply picture the desired end. Get a clear picture of what it would *look* like and what it would *feel* like.

For example, I might picture myself working free of stress and pressure. I am accepting the difficulties of my work with an appetite for challenge knowing that I can enjoy them all and see opportunities for learning in them all. I might envision myself in a totally different work situation and in a position to do much more volunteer work than I am currently able to do. I can envision working confidently and with a sense of purpose that gives sufficient meaning to my efforts. I can also envision better financial returns and different creative accomplishments, knowing that what I am doing is truly making a difference. Getting a clear picture is critical to mobility. The picture can always be changed as you go, but holding the picture is indispensable not only in keeping the desire alive but in providing clarity in steering one's course.

An aphorism that I often heard growing up and that still rings true is "If you don't stand for something, you will fall for anything." If you have a clear vision of where you want to go, you are not as easily distracted by the many possibilities and agendas that could otherwise divert you.

But what about the strength of the desire upon which the picture is based? If mobility is fueled by a mere wish or a "good intention," it has less likelihood of being fulfilled than one based on passion. You can measure the strength of a desire by the obstacles it is capable of overcoming. I once asked a group of participants in a seminar to set goals as if whatever they wished for would be granted. The only condition was that they had to state how much time and effort they would commit in order to make that wish come true. I remember two wishes to this day. The first one was, "I want to be the Southern California karate champion in my weight division. To achieve this, I would be willing to put in six hours of practice a day, five days a week, for the next two years." The next wish was, "I want to live free of stress. I would be willing to put in twenty minutes a day practicing meditation." Some goals are easier to attain than others and thus require less commitment. But you can bet that someone with the passion to dedicate six hours a day to his goal has a great reservoir of fuel for that mobility.

Once you have a clear picture of where you want to go, you can expect things to look different to you in two ways. First, you will be apt to see *more opportunities* to move in your desired direction; at the same time you are likely to be confronted with more obstacles, both inner and outer.

Both are signs that you have begun to move. When you are not moving, you encounter fewer obstacles. When you are moving, the obstacles are visible precisely because you have accepted a goal. In addition, having made the choice to move, you become more alert. The obstacles are more obvious because you are more conscious. If you are too goal oriented, these obstacles can be a source of discouragement and frustration. But you should be happy to see the obstacles because it means you can now find a way to circumvent them and move toward your goal.

EF taught me a very interesting thing about obstacles. He said there were three kinds of people when it comes to facing obstacles. "The first kind of person comes to an obstacle, looks at it, gets discouraged, says, 'That's too much for me,' and gives up. The second kind of person sees an obstacle and says, 'Whatever it takes,

I'll get over it, under it, around it, through it. If I can't do it myself, I'll get tools, help from others, whatever it takes.' " I thought, "Well, that's the type I want to be." EF continued, "The third type of person comes to an obstacle and says, 'Before I try to get beyond this thing, I'm going to try to find a vantage point where I can see what's on the other side. Then if what I see is worth it, I'll do whatever it takes to get over or around the obstacle.' " I realized how often, like Don Quixote, I had done battle with inner and outer obstacles that I didn't really need to fight, but did so just because they were there.

As I move in the desired direction, I am apt to see better ways of moving toward my goal than I could see when I initially started out. This does not mean the steps I took at first were wrong or bad—they may have been the best I could see from that vantage point. If I am not too wedded to my original plan of movement, I may now be able to see better changes to make to get to my destination. I can make changes within my change.

What I can count on is that whatever path I've charted, changes will be needed. This is especially true in today's dynamic work environment. Refraining from planning does not make sense, but being unwilling to make changes in one's plan can be equally disastrous. One of the hardest things about making changes is that you may have been the one who argued so vehemently for the original course. You may have mustered great logic and evidence for its validity. You may have fought a hard battle against others who were proposing a different course. So when the time comes to make a change, it can seem as if you have to admit that you were wrong in the past in order to be correct in the present. Consequently, many companies can't handle major changes without letting go of the leaders who charted the original course. For the same reason, many politicians refuse to make changes in their positions long after those positions are no longer valid. It is not that the original position was wrong at the time, but that it was taken without the benefit of subsequent developments and insights.

I noticed that EF did not have to disparage the past and criticize his original course of action to justify new changes. He simply emphasized the need to make these changes to overcome obstacles and seize new opportunities. I was amazed; it was ingrained in my thinking that the way to motivate change was to criticize the past. Of course, EF was simply practicing the kind of nonjudgmental awareness that I had come to see was so effective in sports.

Change does not have to be viewed as a dialectic between opposing forces out of which some synthesis is hammered. Organic change occurs differently. Crawling is not the wrong way for a child to start moving about. In fact, when the crawling stage is skipped in a rush to start walking, some important developmental changes in the brain are missed. Organic change follows Self 2's natural urges, which may result in movement that meanders like a river, yet somehow finds the path of least resistance to the ocean.

Over the years, I have witnessed many discussions about corporate change. Often they take place in a "black or white, all or nothing" context. Someone proposes a new direction but at the first appearance of difficulty, they are challenged and usually begin to doubt the validity of the whole proposal.

But changes are always required whenever a new direction is taken. No matter how well thought out a major course change may be, it can't anticipate everything. So at the outset of a new change, when uncertainty and risk are at their height, EF would counsel taking steps that are reversible. Then, as confidence grows in the validity of the direction, it is easier to feel confident in making changes within changes without abandoning the direction.

The rewards of being willing to make changes in your changes are great. Some the most successful companies became so only after making radical changes in their products, their means of delivery, their views of their customers and markets, or their own internal organizations and cultures. The hardest yet most powerful changes a company can make are to their "sacred cows"—those people or assumptions that are considered by the culture to be immune from questioning. In his last years as chairman of Coca-Cola, Roberto Goizueta made some of his greatest contributions by trying systematically to identify and challenge all the sacred cows in the company's culture and practices.

The same holds true for individuals. Changes in those assumptions that we didn't even realize were assumptions often lead to the biggest opportunities. For example, for years it had not occurred to me that I had a definition of *work* that was subject to change. I had also assumed that to be an educator I needed to be connected with an educational institution. Getting rid of that assumption revealed rich opportunities that I couldn't have otherwise foreseen. Sometimes it's as simple as changing my definition of what I think my job is, or who I work for, or what my real contribution is, that makes the difference.

Ironically, change itself can become a sacred cow. I have seen some leaders and managers assume that if others are making a certain type of change, then they should. The assumption is that if it's a change, it's good. As EF says, "Random change produces random results." Random changes may not contribute to your mobility. They distract you from movement toward your goals and waste precious time, energy, and resources.

3. **Be Willing to Make Changes within Your Change**—The key here is flexibility. Imagine a tree firmly rooted in the ground that remains pliant enough to bend with the wind without losing its inherent stability. It is the most human of qualities to be firmly committed to what is real and true (the fire within) while remaining unattached to the particular changes that come and go. It is only to the extent that we can grow roots into that part of ourselves that does not change that we are able to be truly flexible and still maintain a true direction.

4. **Keep Your Purpose Clear**—I couldn't believe this step was on EF's list. "Keep your purpose clear"? Just when I'm ready to approach the conclusion, I'm asked to go back to the beginning? But then I realized that in the midst of the actions and reactions that comprise most work, we lose sight of what we are doing it for in the first place. Not only is it difficult to remember the purpose behind our work in general, but even while involved in the details of a

particular task, it is easy to lose sight of why the task at hand was originally undertaken.

When I was playing tennis competitively in state and national tournaments, my coach used to tell me the goal of tennis was simple: "Just win the last point." But that's absurd. If that was really the point of playing the game, all you would have to do is to choose an opponent who was nowhere near as good as you. This would ensure your success every time you played. But that's not the point! Most people choose opponents who are equal to them or better than they are. This is not a good strategy if you want to win the last point, but it is an excellent strategy if you want to have fun and if you want to learn. So we recognize that winning is not the only important thing. But once we're out on the court, in the midst of the match, that understanding can be hard to remember.

The purpose of playing the game and the goal of the game are two different things. When the goal of winning gets confused with the reason for playing—to learn, to enjoy the challenge— then mobility is apt to be compromised. For this reason, the best leaders constantly remind everyone of their primary purpose, even in the midst of the chaos of all the current "emergencies." The wise individual who wants to keep mobile remembers the purpose *behind* whatever changes he decided to make.

Take any specific action you do at work and ask yourself, "Why am I doing this?" Trace the first reason that comes to mind back to the original purpose. How easy is it for you to do this? How clear is the connection? What are the probable consequences of forgetting purpose in the midst of attaining subgoals?

I tried this experiment once with a group of employees at AT&T. Although "customer satisfaction" was expected to be the focus for every single employee, most people couldn't tell me specifically how the work they were doing contributed to this mission. For some hourly employees it was easier because they were directly relating to customers on a daily basis. Some managers found that there were ten to fifteen intermediaries between them and the customer. They were serving people, who served people who eventually "satisfied the customer." It was easy to forget the customer while they simply did their jobs. Or, in other words, they lost sight of the purpose while focused on the subgoals.

But was customer satisfaction really the purpose driving individuals to come work at AT&T? What was on the employees' minds, satisfying the customer or satisfying their immediate supervisors? Neither. None of them had come to work to satisfy either the customers or their supervisors. They had come to work for reasons of self and family—reasons also too often forgotten, and with them the ultimate sense of purpose behind all their hard work.

Why is it so important to remember the primary purpose while accomplishing the subgoals? After all, the "job" can get done whether or not the purpose is kept in mind. So what difference does it really make?

Using the work-equals-performance-minus-interference definition of work, perhaps it doesn't make that much difference. But in terms of mobility, it makes all the difference. Purpose provides both direction and fulfillment. It also provides the foundation for the most important learning.

The answer to this question takes us back to the original concept of mobility. Where do you really want to go? Perhaps you are simply driving your vehicle from paycheck to paycheck. Ask yourself, what are these checks for? Perhaps you will say they are for the quality of life of you and your family. Isn't that closer to your real purpose for working? And if quality of life is the real purpose for working, then wouldn't you want that *while* you were working as well? Wouldn't it make sense to remember that that is what you want while you are pursuing whatever subgoals are involved in your work? And if you didn't remember, how easy would it be to have a rather miserable quality of life while working all for the sake of your quality of life during the short time when you are not working?

It is natural for organizations to want all their employees

aligned behind their organizational goals. Toward this end they articulate mission statements, develop strategies to serve those missions, devise corporate objectives to serve the strategies, and implement projects to fulfill the objectives. There are goals within goals within goals within goals. And keeping the relative priorities of these goals clear is one of the most critical challenges of organizational leadership.

With all the effort that goes into keeping employees focused on the correct priorities, how easy is it for the employees to remember their own individual priorities—not just their part in the organizational work, but *why* they are doing that work in the first place? Who is going to remind them of that? Only the rare manager or leader sees the advantage of doing so. Almost always the individual worker must remind himself.

There is a critical distinction between the *individual's* purpose on one side of the equation and the *organization's* "corporate" mission, strategy, tactics, and goals on the other side. Different individuals can be doing very similar work for very different reasons without there being any conflict in working together. But their primary purposes will eventually take them in different directions: the directions of their individual mobility. The person who works out of fear will move toward fear. The person who works out of responsibility to his family will move toward family. The person who wants to enjoy his life while working will move in the direction of enjoyment.

Finding a Dream House—My sister told me a great story about forgetting purpose in the midst of pursuing goals. She and her husband were trying to buy their first house to accommodate their growing family. Each had his or her own "dream house" in mind. Their search was very frustrating as they went from house to house finding little agreement on what they liked. They looked, discussed, and argued, but could not agree. After several fruitless weeks, my sister said she realized that this was not just a matter of difference of opinion and refusal to compromise, but a matter of not being clear about her purpose. "Why are we looking for a house in the first place?" she asked herself. The answer was obvious. "We are looking for a place where we can live together as a 'happy family.' But we are not moving toward the goal of 'happy family.' If we proceed in this direction, we will be divorced before we find the place to be happy!"

She told her husband that she wanted to stop the search because their relationship meant more to her than the house. This woke her husband up to the irony of the situation, and they both agreed to stop house shopping. A week later, their real estate agent called with "the perfect house." They saw it, both liked it, and bought it without any complications. What had looked impossible when purpose was not clear became relatively effortless once it was.

5. **Keep Your Movement and Direction Synchronized**—Our actions and goals should be consistent with our purpose at all times. But they must not be confused with or allowed to distract from purpose.

This means that if I have made a commitment to my own learning and development as part of my definition of work, then my actions and goals should be in sync with that commitment. I will look for and accept the opportunities that stretch my abilities and understanding. I will continue to make sure that my actions are in line with my performance goals, but I will also set learning goals that are consistent with my desires to develop my capabilities while working. I will learn from experience and not shrink from seeing those mistakes that I can learn from.

The same goes for my commitment to my own enjoyment at work. I have to keep myself from moving in the direction of frustration, pressure, and overload, and move in the direction of satisfaction. Most individuals and companies have a great deal to learn before they can say they have this kind of mobility.

Compromising the inner goals, enjoyment, and growth, is always easy in a culture that values only performance.

An Image of Mobility—I have one image that helps remind me of the value of mobility as distinct from normal goal setting. Two cars—say, two Volkswagens—are about to leave San Francisco for

Chicago. Both are given the same amount of time to deliver their passengers to the destination and both arrive at the same time. But the passenger in the first car arrives tired and stressed after a very bumpy and uncomfortable ride, and the vehicle itself is in need of major repairs before it can take another trip. The second car has a very different trip. Not only does the passenger arrive rested, having enjoyed the entire journey, but the vehicle is in better working order than when it departed. It leaves San Francisco as a Volkswagen and arrives in Chicago as a Mercedes. Both cars accomplish their assigned tasks. But one has gained in capacity and comfort while moving. Both have moved, but only one has mobility. Which car would you rather have on your next trip?

To some people, this image seems fanciful. Cars don't change appreciably in their capabilities while they travel. But what about human beings? We are all drivers of vehicles that are capable of growing in their capacities as they go. Growth is not only possible, but important to us. But growth in capacity without purpose is meaningless. Working free means that I am growing in my capacity to fulfill myself. It means that I continuously increase my capacity to enjoy my life both when working and when not working.

Recognizing the Importance of Mobility—Mobility is the pivotal concept in learning to work free. For many years I believed that simply quieting Self 1 and trusting Self 2 to do the best it could and to learn in the process was sufficient to achieve excellence. I had ample evidence that it worked in sports and many enthusiastic reports from professionals that it worked in a corporate environment as well. There were countless stories about playing out of one's mind and working in a "flow state." I still believe in the unconscious wisdom of Self 2 and I still enjoy being in the flow state whenever it happens, but something needs to be added to the equation to make it complete. That something is mobility.

Mobility is about *conscious* wisdom. It's not just about being in the flow, but about being very clear about where you *are,* where you are *going,* and *why.* In essence, it is about working *consciously.*

To know what you are doing and why requires conscious thought and constant remembrance. It requires being fully awake—aware of all that is happening around you that is relevant to where you are going. Working unconsciously is like being driven in a car without being sure of the destination and without making a conscious choice about which way to turn. It is the difference between driving and being driven. A person who recognizes the importance of mobility is not satisfied with being in *any* flow, it must be in *the* flow of their choice, heading where they want to go.

Mobility of this kind can move me out of the Skinner boxes of conformity. It moves me from being a trained pigeon responding to the bells and lights of my conditioning to an adult human being who chooses freely every step of the way and can move in any direction. I can work alone or in teams without compromising my integrity or direction. Thus, the core of mobility is the recognition that you are totally and unambiguously in charge of your own actions, values, thinking, and goals—in short, your own life.

It is the acceptance of that freedom of choice and the consequent recognition of our responsibility that is so challenging for most of us. The essence of conformity is to abdicate your responsibility to others—to "society," to "upbringing," to environment, past circumstances or events, to "my leader," to "human nature," and more recently to "my genes." This is like blaming your car, which admittedly may have only six cylinders, a dirty windshield, a dented rear end, and needs an oil change, for where you're driving. I am not saying that the vehicles we drive through our work life are not in need of repair. They often require major repairs and they certainly need constant maintenance. But mobility means that I can't blame my car for where it drives me. When I find myself driving in circles, I have to look at who's driving the car. Am I in the backseat being chauffeured through my work life complaining to everyone else about the scenery? To whom did I abdicate the driving? And why?

So if the first step in the Inner Game is to recognize that the vehicle you are driving is capable of movement, the second is to realize that it is *yours,* and to take firm grasp of the steering wheel and begin driving. Changes in direction can always be made, but there is no way to reach freedom at work without accepting full responsibility for where you are and for choosing where you are going.

That's nothing new. But most of us, including myself, need frequent reminders about our power and the responsibility to exercise our mobility. The next chapter presents a tool that has helped me and many others stay conscious at work and keep our hands on the wheels of our respective vehicles.

THE STOP TOOL

The unconscious activity of performance momentum is succinctly satirized in the lyrics of "I'm in a Hurry," made popular by the band Alabama in the early nineties.

> I'm in a hurry to get things done
> Oh, I rush and rush until life's no fun.
> All I really got to do is live and die,
> But I'm in a hurry and don't know why.

Gaining mobility at work can be done. But as attractive and as beneficial as it might sound, it is not easy. Though mobility is a potential for all human beings, and is, I believe, aligned with the very nature of Self 2, most of us work in environments, inner and outer, that make it difficult to achieve.

The hard part is to remain *conscious* while working. When conscious, we see that it is important to us not only to achieve our goals on time, but to achieve them in a way that is satisfying. We see that it is important to enjoy and to learn while we are accomplishing the task at hand. But in the midst of the various pressures, routines, and momentums of our daily work life, it is not so easy to remain truly conscious.

The Inner Game of work is about finding a way of working in which you can be more fully conscious—more aware of where you are, where you are going, and why. This is the essence of mobility and what sets it apart from conformity. It is what Self 2 is all about. It is why redefining work and learning to focus are important. All of this is geared to arriving at a place where we can work more consciously. This is what it takes to work free.

Performance Momentum

Not all movement is mobility. There is a kind of activity that most of us are very familiar with that is not done with conscious intent or awareness of purpose. I call it *performance momentum*. Most of us have habitual actions that we do in the course of a day without a moment's thought for why we do them. We do them because we always do them. I brush my teeth the same way every day and in the same sequence of my morning routine. No problem. I have many routines that do not require being conscious and often it is a relief not to have to give conscious attention to them. The problem comes when my entire day becomes a series of routines or unconscious reactions—when everything I am doing is done in default mode—the momentum that prevails automatically when conscious choice or remembrance of purpose is missing.

Our default mode of working and thinking develops a momentum of its own. The word *momentum* usually refers to the movement of physical objects. They obey the laws of cause and effect and have no choice about it. The billiard ball moves the way it does because it was hit by another ball at a certain speed and direction of impact. We are not being fully human when we allow ourselves to be moved by this sort of reactive momentum. "I got angry and did this because you said that to me" is a "billiard ball" kind of reaction. It implies movement disconnected from conscious purpose. It is Self 1's unconscious, mechanistic way of doing things. Such momentum has movement, often frantic movement, but not mobility. A lot of things may get done, but there is no guarantee that those things will take either the project or the person doing them to successful outcomes.

There are countless examples of momentum in the work arena. Take any situation where someone indicates that there might be a problem. What is the "billiard ball" reaction? Without stopping to evaluate whether this is a problem worth solving, the brain starts generating and debating possible solutions. Not only does it jump into problem-solving activity without thinking about purpose, but it tends to use the same habitual method of problem solving regardless of whether it fits the particular situation at hand. The problem-solving momentum can be so strong that little room is left for creative thinking or strategic perspective. When there has been a mistake, what is the common momentum? Find someone to blame. When blamed, what is the common momentum? Find a way to defend or deflect the blame. When someone gives an opinion, agree or disagree. At work or at play, we set a goal and forget about everything else but reaching that goal. We may still make choices within the momentum, but often we forget the purpose that led us into the activity in the first place. We do it because it has become our default mode, not because we remember *why* we are doing it.

Suppose a request is made of you at work. Some people follow the momentum of automatically saying no, they don't have time. Others follow the momentum of automatically saying yes, without considering whether it relates to their priorities.

Consider the momentum of your to-do lists—putting all the things you "have to do" on a daily list, prioritizing them, and trying to get everything checked off your list by the end of the day. Day after day, you pile the burdens on and try to unload them so that you can pile another set of burdens on the next day. At the end of the day, you are proud of the 149 action items you checked off your list. This can all be done without ever considering the purpose behind a single one of the actions. All you know is "it needs to get done." This is the momentum of the doer. You do do do do do, all day long, call it work, and come home weary and unfulfilled, perhaps irritable, yet somehow proud that you've "worked hard." Perhaps you've kept the demons away for another day. Perhaps you've put out a bunch of fires. But have you advanced the true purpose of your work? And have you enjoyed the process?

A Maserati Without Brakes?—Some people find it very difficult to slow down their thinking momentum, especially when it has been allowed to build. Our minds can easily become like very expensive cars with great engines and accelerators, but poor sets of brakes. When we are running on adrenaline generated by one crisis after another, it can be very hard to find, much less want to apply, the brakes. Yet when driving a car, there are many occasions in which the ability to stop is as important as the ability to go. It's very beneficial to have a mental engine that can do both and that responds to the wishes of the driver. The faster my car, the more important it is that I know how to slow it down.

STOP: The Tool of All Tools

The problem with prescribing any specific remedies for performance momentum is that they can be used only in the specific situations to which they apply. They become too numerous to be remembered and they usually become a substitute for consciousness and clear thinking. I prefer a single tool called STOP. The purpose of STOP is to help a person or team disengage from the tunnel vision of performance momentum, so that mobility and more conscious working can be restored.

Stepping Back from the Sword Fighting in the Valley

I like to introduce the STOP tool using the following analogy. Performance momentum is like being part of a fifteenth-century army fighting off an enemy with swords in a valley between two mountains. While you are engaged in active fighting, your focus is very narrow. You are totally occupied with the immediate threats and opportunities within a few feet of where you are fighting. Perhaps you are fully aware of only the person you are fighting and peripherally aware of one or two potential foes or your compatriots fighting near you. The demands of the immediate situation take all your attention—as well they should.

Now imagine that you take a few moments to disengage from the action and move a few steps up the hillside. Immediately, two things happen. First, you are removed from both the threats and challenges of the fight and all its physical and mental intensity. Second, your perspective has changed. From your more elevated position, you have the advantage of an expanded point of view. Instead of being aware of only a few soldiers, you may be able to see your entire unit. With this improved perspective, you may see where someone needs your help or where there is an advantage to be taken, and you can change your tactics accordingly.

If you allowed yourself the time to take a few more steps up the hillside, your view would be further expanded and perhaps you could view the *tactical* situation of your entire division. And if you went to the very top of the hillside, you could view the entire valley and gain a *strategic* view of both armies at once. The increased disengagement and elevation from the battle would give you a broader perspective and the ability to make more clear-headed choices. If you should conclude that this is a battle worth fighting, you could determine where you could make your best contribution and reengage in the battle with clarity and a renewed sense of purpose.

Thousands of managers from many different companies have agreed that STOP has become an indispensable tool for working effectively. One manager called it the "tool of all tools" because, as he said, "this is the tool that helps you remember to use all the other tools you have in your arsenal." I first heard of STOP from my executive friend, E.F. STOP, as he used it, stood for:

Step back
Think
Organize your thoughts, and
Proceed

Step Back—To step back means to put distance between yourself and whatever you are involved with at the moment. Step back from the momentum of action, emotion, and thinking. Step back and collect yourself. Find a place of balance and poise—a place where you can think clearly, creatively, and independently.

Short STOPs—STOPs can be of any duration. A short STOP may last no more than a couple of seconds. For example, the phone rings while you are working on a project. Your hand reaches out as if of its own volition to answer the phone. A two-second STOP allows you to ask yourself if you really want to answer the phone at this moment. The STOP doesn't imply a correct answer, it just creates the opportunity to put yourself back in the driver's seat. Medium STOPs allow time to reflect and evaluate a situation before proceeding into action. Despite the popular ad that recommends "Just do it," just doing it without stopping to consider options and consequences usually results in a lot of just undoing it. And every once in a while, you can take a big STOP to give yourself the chance to look at issues from a more strategic perspective. This book itself, for example, is an invitation to STOP and take a strategic look at how you are thinking about your work, or any aspect of your life.

Here are some more examples of short to medium STOPs:

- With any communication, STOP before you speak. Is every thought that comes to mind worthy of coming out of the mouth? STOP allows us to screen our thoughts for appropriate content, timing, and conciseness. Similarly, not everything we hear is fit to digest. Use STOP as a filter to discriminate between what is and is not necessary to take to heart.

- You arrive at your desk and notice a few papers that have not been dealt with. Does your hand reach out automatically to pick them up, or do you STOP to consider your priorities for the day first, the most important of which may not be as visible as the papers?

- A fellow worker starts complaining. You know he is the kind of person who likes complaining but never does anything about the problem. He's asking for your agreement with his complaint. Do you STOP or jump in with your opinion without thinking whether or not you want to go down that road with him?

- You find yourself feeling pressured and stressed by your workload, and you realize that in this state you cannot give your best thinking to the task at hand. You know you are making little mistakes. Do you STOP and take a break or "power through"?

- A co-worker is asking you a question. Before he is finished, your mind has already generated an answer to the question you *think* she is framing. Does the answer come out of your mouth before she has finished, or do you stop the mental momentum to fully hear what is being asked and consider your response?

STOP-START-STOP—How many times in a single workday do you have to interrupt what you are doing to start something else? You may even stop something important to take care of a time-sensitive but less important task. In my workday, there can easily be more than twenty such "interruptions." If I'm in my Self 1 performance momentum, each interruption brings an automatic re-action of annoyance and with it a loss of conscious mobility.

The alternative is to first STOP and make a conscious choice about if and when to interrupt what you are doing. This STOP doesn't take away the consequences of the interruption, but allows me to exercise my choice, which removes the annoyance and provides a sense of freedom and enjoyment because I still have my hands on the steering wheel of my work day. If I decide yes, then before starting the new activity, I take a short STOP to consciously "close the books" on the last activity and to orient myself to the purpose and context of the next. Creating a sense of closure on each activity and making a conscious choice about the next relieves the mind from carrying an accumulating burden of unfinished tasks. It can make all the difference between a satisfying day of conscious choices and what otherwise could feel like a fatiguing day of needless interruptions. The trick is to realize you don't have to carry unfinished tasks in your mind; you can lay them down, knowing they will be there when you have the chance to pick them up again.

Here are just a few of the benefits from practicing STOP-START-STOP:

- More acknowledgment of work accomplished
- Fewer work burdens carried home at the end of the day
- More conscious choices made
- Feeling more rested and energized during and after work
- More innovation available
- A clearer sense of purpose and priority
- More conscious changes made where needed
- Remembering one's learning goal
- Checking on feeling levels—enjoyment, stress, tiredness
- Remembering forgotten commitments
- Deciding whether a longer STOP is needed

The benefits are many. But how do you find the discipline to do it?

The STOP Bell—Recently, I was explaining STOP to a person who periodically goes on a retreat (a long STOP) at a monastery where everyone has different tasks to perform during the day. At irregular intervals, a bell is sounded, indicating that everyone should stop whatever they are doing for two minutes. There is no instruction what to do other than simply to stop working.

"At first it was the hardest thing to be asked to suddenly stop doing what you were doing for no apparent reason," she said.

"What did you find so hard about it?" I asked with somewhat feigned naïveté.

"Well, I used to hate it whenever I heard the bell," she said, gritting her teeth. "I hated having to stop the momentum of doing—especially at someone else's request. But during those two minutes, we would take a deep breath, center ourselves, and soon find that our awareness would expand as well as our appreciation for the work we'd accomplished. We began to regard it as one of the hardest but most beneficial of the disciplines we did."

Short STOPs take very little time but pay big dividends. Each one reminds you that you are not a victim of performance momentum, but someone who can stop, think, and start again by choice. This is a valuable habit to develop for anyone on the journey of working consciously.

Creating Think Space—It can be useful to create a distinct physical and mental environment that is conducive to reflective or strategic thinking. You can choose a particular chair, or a particular room, or any environment that you can go to repeatedly. This helps slow you down and prepares you for reflective, conscious thinking. This is creating "think space."

Think space must be sufficiently disengaged from the mental and emotional performance momentum. Imagine yourself in the *captain's chair* from which you can view all the important components of your situation. You *are* the Captain Kirk of your own spacecraft. You have all of your human potentialities and sensory, mental, and emotional intelligence, as well as all of your developed qualities and capabilities available to you. Picture yourself in the control room, where you have every kind of viewing equipment at your disposal. You can zoom in on any part of the situation to see the detail or zoom out to view the big picture. You are aware of the many other human resources available to you for getting more information, expertise, or assistance. In this chair, you view all events with the detachment of someone committed to the integrity of the entire ship and its mission, yourself, and your commitment.

My friend Alan Kay, who is often referred to as one of the fathers of the personal computer, is a reflective thinker of the highest order. He often tells audiences, "Point of view is worth eighty IQ points." Think space is a way of establishing a different point of view from which to do your thinking and gain the benefit of whatever added intelligence comes your way.

Think—To stop thinking momentum in order to think may sound like a paradox, but it is not. There is a shift in the thinking gears, a disengagement of thought in order to either rest or engage in a different level of thinking.

Below are some questions that I find very helpful in focusing the powers of thought and reminding myself of the elements of mobility. These questions are a great place to start once you've established your think space:

- What am I (we) trying to accomplish?
- What purpose is being served?
- What agenda is being followed—where did it come from?
- What is the priority here?
- Is there a change needed? In direction? In definition?
- Is movement in sync with direction?
- What are the likely consequences?
- What are the critical variables?
- What's missing?
- Is the problem I am working on the real problem?
- What do I really want?
- What's at stake?

- Am I enjoying work? Am I moving in a fulfilling manner?
- How does this look from the point of view of other key people?
- What assumptions am I making?
- What resources could I access that I am not?
- What's my prevailing attitude?

It's not a bad idea to have the questions that work for you visible somewhere within your physical think space. Many of the managers who have found benefit in using the STOP tool have a red stop sign in their office. Such reminders are useful for keeping you conscious and mobile.

Organize Your Thoughts—Thinking does not usually occur in a perfectly organized fashion. Especially in longer STOPs where there has been creative thinking about problem solving or strategic planning, there is always the task of bringing order to your thoughts before you are ready to proceed. But to "organize" is your chance to pull your thinking together, bring coherence to your plan, consider priorities, and provide a sequence for actions. It is the necessary preparation before taking up the sword again and descending from think space into the battle.

Proceed—You don't stay on the mountaintop if you want to take action. There is definitely a right time to descend from your think space, and that is when the brain has been refreshed and clarified. When the purpose and the next steps are clear, and you feel more connected with yourself and your motivations, you are ready to go back to work. You continue with actions until the clarity fades or you again need rest.

Resistance to STOPs

It is wise to anticipate resistance to using the STOP tool, coming from both yourself and others in your work team. The biggest resistance will come from performance momentum. If you are a go, go, go person, there is a natural resistance to STOPs. Of course, the more you hate to STOP, the more important it probably is. I sometimes think it is part of Self 1's nature to be a nonstop thinking machine always wanting something to chew on. Yet it's also true that our best and most creative thinking usually comes when our minds are quiet and relatively relaxed, and it often comes when least expected. Creative people have learned to keep notepads by their beds and showers for this reason.

But there is a more profound reason for the resistance to STOPs. Stepping back makes you more conscious. It's like turning on the lights in a dark room. You see things that maybe you would just as soon not see. Your own mistakes become more visible, as well as obstacles you've been denying, either in yourself or in team members. The Self 1 part of us, in spite of its critical nature, enjoys the dimmer light, where certain things can remain hidden and not confronted. It's hard to admit that we sometimes prefer the darkness to the light, but it's a common experience to find ourselves periodically in the dim light of semiconsciousness.

Besides, STOPs take time, and we all know we don't have enough time. Time is not the reason we resist STOPs, but it is the most frequently used rationalization. Anyone who has used STOP realizes that it takes minutes and saves hours. Still, we resist it when it is most needed. The only way to really know when to use and not to use this tool is by starting to use it.

When to Use STOP

One vice president who was telling me how big a difference the STOP tool had made for him ended his remark by saying, "The only problem is that when I need to use it the most, I forget to use it." Below are eight occasions when it can be most useful to utilize the STOP tool for working consciously.

1. **STOP at the Beginning and End of Each Workday**—Nature itself provides time for STOPs at the beginning and end of every day, and many cultures recognize the value of a midday break. I recom-

mend giving yourself a chance to step back and think about what's important on at least three occasions during the day, even if just for a few minutes each.

Starting the day with a STOP gives you a better chance of working consciously during the day. Sleep is a natural "stepping back." Between the time of waking and the start of the day's activities, you have a rare opportunity to gain perspective on what is important to you, at least for that day.

If I don't take a few minutes to establish my priorities at that time, there is no doubt that the urgencies of everything else will control the day. This is my time to remember that it is my life, to grant myself mobility, and to get in touch with the direction that comes from my felt desire. It's important for me to do this before I let my mind jump into problem solving or thinking about "all the things I have to do today." I also make notes on this STOP so that I can refer to them at STOPs during the day. It may help to hold this STOP somewhere other than in your work environment. Take a walk or do it over coffee. Whatever you choose, let it be an environment that is as free as possible from distraction.

Checking in with a STOP once or twice during the day to see how you are doing on your original set of priorities allows you the chance to get back on course, to make changes within your change, or to remember your purpose.

A STOP at the end of the workday can be as valuable as one at the beginning. The first step is to make a clear decision *when* you are ending the workday. If you decide it ends at the workplace, usually a wise choice, then when you leave, close the door on your work so you don't carry the work, your burdens, your roles, or your frustrations home with you in your briefcase or in your mind. The purpose of this STOP is to fully complete your workday so that you can be fully available for your non-work life. If you do choose to take work home, decide beforehand just how long you are going to give to it and when. Practice STOP-START-STOP. Don't let work take over the rest of your life, because it will if you don't stop it.

Make it a learning goal to look back and "debrief" the day.

What has been accomplished? What went wrong? What didn't? What could be learned? This STOP takes some courage. It is one thing to look forward at the beginning of the day to all I plan to accomplish, but it can be quite another to become aware of the gap between what I hoped for and what I actually accomplished. To take advantage of this STOP, don't let the Self 1 critic into your think space. Practice nonjudgmental awareness. Looking back at "what stood out" at the end of the day can improve the quality of the next day by allowing Self 2 to do its magic, selecting what's important and what might need some attention.

One final note on these daily STOPs: Sharing the appropriate content of these STOPs with team members, spouses, or partners can go a long way to providing mutual respect and cooperation. It also gives everyone involved a renewed sense of purpose and a greater chance at mobility.

2. STOP at the Beginning and End of Any Work Project—Perhaps it is obvious to say that a team or individual should STOP at the beginning of any project, large or small. But there is usually such a momentum to begin the action that the time for envisioning, planning, and research is cut short. In performance-oriented environments, the steps of mobility are neglected and work tends toward the unconscious default modes of business as usual. It is right to value action, but not at the expense of prudent forethought. The consequence of not taking a STOP is that you will generate more actions than are necessary, as well as mistakes that take more action and time to correct. Conscious work aims to get to the desired destination with the least action possible, not the most.

STOPs at the beginning of a project are times to gather needed information, consider alternative solutions and strategies, and examine available resources. These activities are often considered "not getting anything done." To question the initial assumptions brought to the project, or how the project may or may not be in sync with purpose, or how it relates to other ongoing projects, is also considered "thinking" and therefore not real work.

The longer and more important the project, the more important it is to step back to gain perspective. Sufficient thought must be given to alternatives and consequences, these thoughts must be organized into a plan, and the plan must include a way to make further changes to the plan.

STOPs at the end of a project give you a chance to bring the project to completion, celebrate the accomplishments, and consider what can be learned that may benefit future projects. Sports teams have made a habit of this kind of debriefing and often pore over videotapes of individual and team performances to maximize their learning. In most work settings, when people are apt to feel that the project took longer than expected, they feel they don't have the time or the stomach for a debriefing. They don't consider that the project took too long because they hadn't sufficiently learned the lessons of previous projects. A good debriefing is capable of saving exponential amounts of time on future projects. The hardest part is developing the habit in the face of the momentum to get on to whatever is next.

3. STOP to Make a Conscious Change—Something unexpected has occurred; a new fact has been introduced into the situation; an unforeseen opportunity or issue has arisen; a change in plans is called for. A change STOP creates a space for making a conscious change instead of rushing ahead with the first reaction that comes to mind. It's difficult to evaluate a need for a change in the midst of performance momentum. It's common to make a change just for the sake of change. It's easy to make a change that looks like a good idea, but can unwittingly have a disastrous effect on other elements of the situation. It is easy to ignore the need for change STOPs because of time pressure, attachment to the original plan, uncertainty about the best course of action, stress, and tiredness. All of these contribute to the unconscious momentum that STOPs help overcome.

Change STOPs can be used for minor adjustments to the plan or major changes in direction. Sometimes they are triggered not by a change in the external environment, but by an innovative idea about how to improve the quality of processes or results.

Here are a few questions that can focus thought for a change STOP:

- Is this a random change or a purposeful one?
- What is driving the proposed change?
- Do the benefits outweigh the costs?
- Are the people involved capable and ready to make the change?
- Have alternative changes been considered?
- Is the proposed change in sync with direction?
- Who or what will be affected by this change?
- What communications are necessary?
- What is the best time, place, and means for these communications?
- What can or should be learned before attempting this change?

Change STOPs can be used not only to access change in action plans, but to examine assumptions or critical definitions used in one's work. The renowned businessman Robert W. Woodruff, who was president of the Coca-Cola Company from 1923 to 1949, wanted to make a change in the way his entire sales force related to customers. He wanted them to be less sales oriented and more service oriented. To initiate this change, he designed a change STOP that has become famous. He called the sales force together and fired them all. Then he announced that he was hiring service personnel starting the next morning and that all were welcome to apply. What Woodruff was trying to accomplish was not merely a new sales strategy, but a new way for salespeople to look at themselves and their roles. He was redefining selling. A simple but profound change of that nature, because it is a change in context, can automatically provoke thousands of changes in behavior and attitude.

Change STOPs are opportunities not just for considering needed changes, but for letting go of outmoded ways of doing things. Woodruff knew, as do all good managers, that the most difficult thing about making change is not so much the learning of new ways of behaving as the unlearning of old ways of behaving. The failure of most changes can be attributed to a lack of awareness of the default modes (unconscious momentum) governing current practices. It's difficult to make a change when you aren't sufficiently aware of how you are doing something in the present. A major lesson of the Inner Games of tennis and golf was that once you become aware of current behaviors or thought patterns, change becomes relatively effortless.

4. STOP to Address Mistakes—The best people make mistakes and mistakes can be costly. They can also be important learning experiences. Of course, it is nice to anticipate mistakes and avoid them when possible, but the biggest problems come when mistakes aren't even recognized. If the work environment is overly judgmental of mistakes and the people who make them, then mistakes will be *less* likely to be noticed and responded to. When I was an officer in the navy, it was common practice for all junior-ranking officers to keep their superiors from finding out about failures. Avoiding bad performance reviews or a "chewing out" was more important than ship efficiency and sometimes even took priority over safety concerns. In corporations, I have found a similar creativity when it comes to ignoring and covering up mistakes, both task related and interpersonal.

The value of creating a nonjudgmental work environment is that mistakes can be seen and dealt with when they occur. A "breakdown STOP" can be called whenever either the task or team integrity has been compromised.

Here are some of the questions that can be used to focus a breakdown STOP:

- What was the commitment that led the action, event, or result to be called a mistake? Example: The mistake was that Tom didn't pass on a particular piece of information to Martha, which led Martha to make a misrepresentation to a valued customer. The commitment that made Tom's mistake a mistake was a team promise to keep one another informed and an understanding that all team members were responsible for customer satisfaction. Remembering the commitment behind the mistake allows the mistake to become the occasion for everyone involved to reaffirm the commitment.

- Who accepts responsibility for the mistake? In a judgmental working culture, one of Self 1's favorite and most costly games is "the blame-credit game." The goal is to accept as little blame as possible for what goes wrong and to get as much credit as possible for what goes right. It's time-consuming and it deprives participants of the use of a great many brain cells that might otherwise contribute to their mobility. Instead of playing this game, a breakdown STOP can be used for each person to consider *accurately* just what part he played in the mistake. The purpose is not to assign blame more accurately, but to make learning from the mistake accurate and appropriately distributed. Tom, for instance, might discover that the mistake behind his failure to inform Martha was a conflict in priorities that needed to be resolved. Martha might discover that she could have been more proactive in getting the needed information from Tom.

What was the *real* mistake? Often the mistake was not a mistake at all. The real mistake may have been several cause-and-effect steps behind what was finally noticed. The breakdown STOP can be used to consider the true cause of the apparent mistake and this is a powerful learning opportunity. For example, it might reveal that Tom and Martha are overloaded, and without a break, both will be unproductive and prone to more mistakes. Another scenario is that a relatively small mistake can reveal a very costly mistake just waiting to happen. Tom might be about to lose the account that he is working on and is using the lack of communication from Martha to avoid facing this reality. By being willing not to cover up the "small" mistake, the breakdown STOP can be used to avert the potentially grave mistake.

5. STOP to Correct Miscommunication—A communication STOP should be called when adequate communication is missing or when miscommunication has occurred. I have asked thousands of people what they see as the biggest problem they face at work. Failure to communicate is perhaps the most common complaint. Upper-level managers say they are not heard by middle-level managers; hourly employees claim they are not heard by their supervisors; middle managers believe they aren't heard either by upper-level managers or by lower-level managers. Of course, everyone claims to be speaking clearly, but no one is hearing correctly.

Miscommunication causes a breakdown in trust. Calling a communication STOP gives everyone a chance to step back from the pressures that may have provoked the miscommunication in the first place, get a little emotional distance from its consequences, make some ground rules about not engaging in blame games, and create an environment for straight and tactful speaking and listening.

Here are some questions to help focus your communication STOPs:

Re: Speaking
- What do I really want to say? To whom?
- Is what I am saying in sync with my purpose?
- What kind of communication is this—a report, an opinion, a proposal, a complaint, an expression of feeling, an insight, feedback?
- What assumptions or hidden messages lie behind what I am saying?

- How can I expect the listener to interpret what I have to say?

Re: Listening
- What's the message behind the message?
- What's the feeling behind the message?
- What am I listening for?
- What kind of response is being called for?

6. STOP to Learn or Coach—A learning STOP can be done alone or with a coach. Athletes have an accepted practice of taking STOPs in the action for the sake of learning or coaching. These stops, called time-outs, are very rare in the culture of business. As a result, there tends to be less conscious practice of skills and less effective development of individual and team capabilities.

Formalizing learning and coaching STOPs is a relatively easy way to activate the learning side of the work triangle. Sometimes it takes just a moment before starting an activity to ask yourself a question that will provide a focus for learning. Once the convention of such STOPs is accepted, a coach can perform his function in less than a minute. It may take no more than asking a single question or offering a critical variable to focus attention.

Obviously, there are times for longer learning STOPs, extended coaching conversations, off-site seminars or training. But as I pointed out earlier, the greatest seminar is your workday itself, and all you need to do to turn it into a valuable experience is to enroll in it as a student. Doing this is as simple as taking three learning STOPs—one at the beginning of the task or project, one midway, and one to debrief at the end. We'll talk more about coaching and learning STOPs in the next chapter.

7. STOP to Rest—Breaks or rest STOPs are unlike the others in that after you stop working and step back, there is nothing to think about or organize. The point is simply to rest and allow the brain and body to rejuvenate. If you have been sitting down to work, it is a good idea to get up and allow your body a chance to

stretch and move. Rest STOPs don't have to be long. Frequent one-minute breaks can do wonders; longer, less frequent breaks for coffee or lunch are common. But for a break to count as a rest STOP, it has to really be restful. If, during your STOP, you jump right into a work-related conversation, it doesn't count. You are still working and haven't yet taken your break.

The value of rest STOPs is greatly underrated in performance-oriented cultures. Such breaks seem to be the antithesis of performance. But rest STOPs are essential for mobility and optimal performance. Used properly, they actually help people make more effective use of time. Of course, no one "has time" for rest breaks. It is when you think you don't have time that rest STOPs are the most important. It is when the brain is under high demand and not given a chance to relax that mistakes are most likely. The amount of time it takes to correct such mistakes is likely to be much greater than the sum of all break time. So it comes down to the choice of how to use your time. Not only do rest STOPs optimize your working capacity, they remind you that you, not "the pressure," are in charge of how you use your time.

Work Free of Stress—Some experts think stress a positive and necessary factor in the workplace. I have never understood the validity of this point of view. The traditional and commonsense definition of the word *stress* pertains to the pressure exerted on a body that causes it to strain or deform itself. Stress triggers huge changes in our nervous systems, known as the "fight or flight response." Medical research tells us that when the fight/flight mechanism is being constantly triggered in the workplace, it puts a huge demand on all the systems in the body, including the immune system. Working for long periods in such a state not only puts us at greater risk of physical breakdown, but compromises our higher mental capacities as well. It is well documented that the brain under stress can remember less well, is less creative, and develops tunnel vision (or narrowed awareness). None of these are good for mobility, for attaining external goals, or finding a means of work that is satisfying. It is also well documented, and true to most people's personal experience, that some of our most creative thoughts come during breaks and when least expected—such as when taking a shower or a walk.

I work in a team with two physicians who are exploring the relationship between disease and stress. They tell me that there is growing evidence of this relationship and that the kinds of pressures many of their patients are facing in the workplace put demands on the immune system, which makes one more vulnerable to a number of common health problems. Their research shows that many people under high levels of stress are not aware of it. The anxiety and corresponding adrenaline rush experienced in the body make it more difficult for people to be aware of the subtler signals their bodies are sending. When we repeatedly choose to override our bodies' signals to take a break, we soon lose the ability to recognize these signals at all. Patients are surprised to find themselves close to the edge of exhaustion, resulting in a breakdown of physical or mental functioning. Prevention of such stress levels includes many of the things we have been discussing in this chapter—staying in charge of your work, staying conscious of your body as well as of the degree of demand and burden you are accepting, and taking frequent and real breaks.

In the domain of work, I define stress as a pressure or force that threatens the balance or inner stability of the worker. When a suspension bridge or any of its girders is under too much pressure or tension, it can lose resilience and break. For me, mobility means working stress free. I see no need to accommodate stress or try to manage it. Stress is a signal to me that I am no longer in control of my way of moving at work. Besides, whether or not I am working under time constraints, and usually I am, I work better and more consciously when I am not stressed. It is also much more enjoyable. In my experience, the most injurious stress comes from Self 1. Self 2 doesn't need the stuff except in rare circumstances when it requires adrenaline and other hormones to deal with a temporary emergency. People who put Self 1 in the driver's seat work in a constant state of emergency and don't believe they can get anything done without it. This belief spreads crisis-consciousness to team members and heightens stress levels. You may have very little control over the stress levels of those around you or their stress-producing behaviors, but you can make a commitment to yourself to keep your own head cool, collected, and conscious. This is the underlying purpose of all the STOPs.

Use STOP to Build Inner Stability—Mobility is an entirely different response to challenge than the fight/flight momentum. The inherent goal of the body is to retain homeostasis or balance. Stability and balance are requirements of mobility. I believe a much better strategy than "managing stress" is "building stability." The greater the stability, the more pressure one can withstand without losing balance. Use rest STOPs to build inner stability and strengthen the resilience of Self 2. External demands are inevitable. Giving Self 2 what it needs to build stability is the best way to ensure that you can withstand pressures when they come without losing balance. Building stability is important to your mobility whether you feel stress at the moment or not.

Stress is not the only signal that it is time for a rest STOP. Another signal is feeling that "working just isn't fun anymore"— when the next project looks more like a burden than an opportunity, when "have to" is overcoming "want to." Enjoyment is both a right and an opportunity for human beings. Working consciously means moving through working days in a satisfactory state of enjoyment. There is no reason to accept less—at least for the long run.

Sometimes what you need is a change, not just a rest. The work you are doing may be okay, but the physical or social environment may not be. It may seem self-centered not to just grit your teeth and bear a certain amount of misery while working. I don't buy it. During a STOP, I can reflect on how much I am contributing to my misery. That should definitely be the first step. But if, in the final analysis, the work itself or the work environment needs to be changed, you must summon the courage to make that change. Some of the most successful people I know have made such choices and wound up in work that they were better suited to and enjoyed more.

Don't forget that a STOP is for the purpose of going; the tool is designed to serve mobility. And the aim of mobility is to move consciously so that both inner and outer goals are fulfilled. Without STOPs, we are much more likely to be the victims of unconscious momentum and blind conformity. One final word: Design your STOPs to be user friendly. If you let Self 1 impose them on you as a "should," you miss the benefit they can bring. Build your STOPs gradually as you realize their benefit to you, and don't become overly analytical about them.

8

THINK
LIKE A CEO

I have a computer software package that allows you to view details of almost every street, road, and highway in the United States. At the most detailed level, you can call up a map that shows where on a specific street any particular address is located. At the broadest level, you view a map of the entire United States. To go from the view of my home street, to a view that includes all the streets of my town, to a map of Los Angeles, to one of the western United States, and finally to the broadest view takes twenty "step backs." And still, I can see only the United States.

The human brain has this same capability of stepping back or focusing in to allow you to view something from the broadest possible perspective to a narrow focus with great detail. There are times when you want to take "a big STOP" to view your entire life from a place where you can see everything without limitation of a particular space or time. It is from such a vantage point that you can gain the perspective to reflect on the larger or most fundamental questions.

At some point, taking a big STOP is essential to gaining mobility. Core values can be clarified and recommitted to. It provides a time for getting clear on the purpose that gives direction to all of your other purposes and for making any changes that will help you fulfill your most important goals.

Creating an appropriate "think space" for a big step back is not always easy. Often we are so entangled in the mental and emotional frameworks of our current situations that we can't easily find a way to step back out of them and see other possibilities. Sometimes it takes a crisis such as being fired, the death of someone close to us, or a life-threatening disease to bring us to the point of examining what our lives are all about. Many people who survive these crises end up greatly valuing the new thinking and perspective on life that they have gained as a result.

Taking a big STOP is an alternative to waiting for such a crisis to provoke fundamental reappraisal of your values, commitments, and perspective. Most crises can be *imagined* and doing so can help you get into a useful think space. "Yes, I could be downsized." It might be an advantage to consider this before it happens. What would you do? What kind of work environment would you look for? What would be important to you in making the decisions that you would face? Your answers to such questions might be very valuable to you even if you don't get downsized.

Or, if you are more daring, consider the possibility that your doctor tells you that you have a condition that will greatly shorten your life span and allow you only a few years of productive work. How would your thinking about work change?

These gloomy scenarios are not for the purpose of contingency planning, but to bring into focus the changeability of our circumstances and the preciousness of the limited time we have. This perspective eludes most of us while we're involved in our day-to-day lives.

Who Is the Most Important Person in a Corporation?

My executive friend had another way to provoke strategic thinking. During one of my tennis court conversations with him, he asked me a simple question. "Who do you think is the most im-

portant person in a corporation?" I was about to say "the CEO,"
when he went on to say, "I think each one is the most important."

I was familiar with the theory that a chain is only as strong as
its weakest link. I had even espoused it. And I could think of circumstances in which any person who did something really stupid
could bring down the entire corporation. Nonetheless, I knew I
would consider it more important to consult with the CEO than
with the janitor.

But then I realized that EF had not asked who is most important to the organization—just who is most important. I had been
conditioned by my culture to believe that "all people were created
equal" but not that all people were equally *important.* EF then
asked if any person in the organization was more important than
the organization itself. Gradually it dawned on me that he was not
comparing the relative importance of people or groups, but making a distinction between the inherent value of any human being
compared to an artificial entity called an organization. I realized
how easily I had come to place importance on organizations over
the people that were in them. An organization is not as important
as any person in it, because an organization is not made up of
people, it is simply an agreement among people. If IBM were dis-
banded tomorrow, all the employees and shareholders would still
be alive. When I looked at it one way, any major company seemed
very big, very important, and very long lasting. It had traditions,
know-how, and wealth. But looked at from the other perspective,
is all of that worth a single human existence? To EF, the answer
was clear.

You Are the CEO of an Amazing Corporation—EF said he viewed every
single living person as the CEO of a corporation of incomparable
value. As such, each had very important decisions to make. The
corporation he was talking about was the human being. He then
asked me what *product* I had decided to produce with my corporation. I had never really thought about it in that light and I decided
to take a big STOP.

We Have All Won the Lottery—I began to take stock of my "corporate resources." As I looked at everything that was involved in simply being human, I realized that this corporation was not at all insignificant. I also felt a growing sense of responsibility and autonomy. As CEO of this incredible instrument, I reported to no one. I found the exercise gave me an invaluable perspective on my ultimate mobility and soon I designed a module of an executive seminar based on it. I invite you to participate in the basic elements of this module. It starts with a simple question, totally out of any particular context: "Who do you work for?"

Participants give responses that range from "my boss," "the company," "the president," to sarcastic responses such as "my wife," "my kids," "the dog." But some corporate executives give another answer: "I work for myself."

At this point, I declare that my objective is that by the end of the module, everyone will be self-employed. A few eyebrows are raised, and I make it clear that this is not as easy as simply quitting one's corporate job. I ask the participants to take a big step back and to use their imagination.

Imagine that one day you win a lottery. In this lottery, the prize is not money, but a corporation. What you are handed is the name of the company, ABC, its address, the key to the headquarters office, and an official document assuring you that you are the owner and CEO. You go to the address, an impressive building with the name of the corporation on the outside. You find your way to the CEO's office and sit down in your chair. You know nothing yet about this corporation that you now own other than that you are the CEO and fully responsible for all future decisions. What are you going to do?

Everyone tends to have a similar approach. They know that their first order of business is to learn all they can about their new companies. Although priorities for this learning vary, most agree that they would find out about the products or services being produced, the market, the human and physical resources, the earnings, the financial assets, etc.

Then they list things like major strategies, mission statements, values, policies, organizational structures, and the software. I remind each CEO that he is now in a position to change anything. "If any of the people, policies, strategies, values, mission statements, even products, are not to your liking, you can make changes. You can disband the entire company, expand it, or keep it the way it is."

Then I ask, "What is the root meaning of 'corporation'?" Usually someone knows that it comes from the Latin word *corpus*, meaning "body." "Imagine then that the corporation you have won in the lottery is not a business, but a human body. You are very happy as soon as you hear the news because you realize you have been "incorporated" in the Rolls-Royce of all bodies. After all, you could have gotten the body of a grasshopper, a rhinoceros, a bluebird, or an ant. You ended up with the top of the line, and you are the owner and CEO. What are you going to do?"

Taking Stock of Inner Resources—What is the "hardware" with which every human being is born? I ask my seminar participants to catalog the most important "inner equipment" they have inherited as the proud owner of their company. The first "resources" they usually acknowledge are physical, including the senses, body parts, and the brain. Is this "expensive" equipment? What is its replacement value? How long was it in research and development before reaching its current level of evolution? I remind them to consider the assets of their corporations without comparing them to any other corporations.

What capabilities are inherent to every human being? There is the ability for language, reason, intuition, creativity, and imagination. Very expensive equipment! Very advanced after aeons in research and development. What other qualities and attributes are part of the potential of being human? It takes a little courage to do this cataloging without listening to Self 1 say, "But I don't have this or that quality." But the fact is that if you can see it in any human being, you have it, too, in some stage of development.

Here are some of the inner resources listed by seminar participants as belonging to the hardware of the human corporation. Which of these would *you* include as part of your own corporation? Are there others you would add?

Emotions
Conscience
Appreciation
Wonder
Joy
Happiness
Gratitude
Peace
Love
Beauty
Satisfaction
Fulfillment
Ecstasy
Harmony
Tranquillity
Meaning
Purpose
Choice
Trust
Consciousness
Respect
Humor

Now ask yourself these questions:

- How much access do you have to each of these resources?
- How much access do you want?
- Which have you developed and which do you ignore?
- Who is deciding how they will be used?

- Have you established a clear mission statement for this corporation?
- Do you have clear policies, values, priorities?
- If so, who made them?
- When were they last reviewed by you?
- How are the operating decisions made for this corporation?
- Do you feel in a position to make any changes you would like in mission, values, policies, priorities?

The CEO of any corporation would ask such questions as a matter of course. But do we do the same for ourselves? If not, why not? Is it that a legal entity is considered more important than an individual human being? Or is it that we don't feel quite the same sense of autonomy and responsibility for this human corporation as we would if we were actually the CEOs of our own companies?

How Many Shares in Your Corporation Do You Still Own?—In corporations, the big decisions are made by the major shareholders. How are the shares of your corporation distributed? Have you sold some shares to others, who now have a vote in your decisions? Have you become a minority shareholder in your own company?

Take a moment to write down your answers to these and the following questions. Shares are defined as voting rights in decisions that you make about your life. Selling shares means you have to get approval by someone else before you can make *your* decisions. It does *not* mean you have sold shares if you have made autonomous decisions with other CEOs to work together or even to work for someone else. The issue is whether your individual autonomy has been compromised.

In my seminars, some high-ranking corporate executives report that they control as little as 10 percent of the shares of their corporations. Others report as much as 100 percent. The median is just a little over 50 percent. In most cases, I feel that the most honest and insightful executives realize that they have sold more shares than they would have liked to believe.

To Whom Did You Sell Shares and for What?—Answers vary. One is "I sold for approval or acceptance." Another is "to avoid conflict or punishment." Other answers include "love," "money," "protection," "certainty," "power," "success," "control," "belonging," "sex," "friendship." One person said, "I've sold shares in my corporation for shares in certain other people's corporations. I think we have traded shares!" Many people in the seminar laughed and nodded.

Can You Buy Back Shares?—I stipulate one ground rule that is slightly different from corporate stock law. In the case of the human corporation, if the original CEO and owner has at least one share of stock left, he has it in his power to buy back any or all of his original shares. This is a special privilege granted to you at birth along with your right to sell shares. What does it cost to buy back shares? You have to pay in the same denomination that you sold them for. If you sold shares for approval, you may risk the withdrawal of that approval when you buy them back. If you sold them for friendship, you might risk losing the "friend."

Do You Want Your Shares Back?—How many of the sold shares do you want back? If you have only a minority position, how do you feel about that? Some people feel okay about it because it makes them feel less responsible for the condition of their lives. Frankly, I recognize that questionable logic in myself and think it takes some courage to admit it. For others, it doesn't take courage; they simply don't want the responsibility.

Who Is on Your Board of Directors?—Most people, however, want to buy back some of their outstanding shares. I suggest that they do so at their next board of directors meeting. Who is on the board? Think about whether you have organized your life into departments, each having its own director. There may be a director of finance, of public relations, of family affairs, career development, recreation, religion, values, community service. Are your parents on the board? Your boss? Your spouse or partner? These board members may not always see eye to eye and some are more loyal to external shareholders than to you. As CEO, your job is to get the best possible alignment behind your vision and get as many of these departments synchronized as possible.

Holding a Board of Directors Meeting—Seminar participants are then given an hour to hold an imaginary board of directors meeting. The CEO makes all decisions about what is on the agenda.

Possible agenda topics include:

- Outstanding shares? Possible decision to buy back.
- Product line. What is it now? Any changes?
- Primary mission statement. Origin? Needs clarification?
- Life priorities.
- Evaluation of mobility.
- Redefining needed? Self? Work? Relationships?
- Any important issues being avoided?
- Regular board meetings? Time and agenda for next one.

In seminars where I have compared the percentage of outstanding shares before the board meeting to that of a week later, there has been a significant increase in the percentage of shares owned by the CEOs. A shift from below 50 percent to over 70 percent is not unusual. This increase comes in spite of the fact that there are usually a few people who initially claimed they had more than 80 percent of their shares, but who decrease that estimate considerably after closer review.

I have seen some executives whose most difficult challenge was to buy back shares from family members. Still others felt they had many outstanding shares owned by deceased parents. Others had sold them to organizations, causes, or institutions. It is not always easy to buy back shares. But there is much to be gained from the reduction of inner conflict and the increase in mobility that can result. Some people have told me that they could not remember ever having spent an hour alone when they weren't "doing" something. They had been too busy taking care of all their shareholders! The board meeting was a valued experience to consider what was most important to them.

There was one female executive from California who shared with me the results of taking this exercise to heart. During her one-hour board meeting, she came to the conclusion that there were too many people thinking that they owned shares in her company. Some were family members; some were co-workers. She realized that she had some serious buying back to do and spent the better part of a weekend deciding just whom she had sold shares to and what for, and how she was going to give the message to each shareholder that he no longer had voting rights. She understood that there was an important distinction between the right to give an opinion and the right to vote. She also knew that taking these stands with her former shareholders was liable to come as a surprise. Especially from family members, she knew she could expect initial resistance and subsequent testing of her new policies. I spoke to her several weeks after these conversations were complete to ask her how everything was. She said it had been a real shock both to her and her former shareholders, but the results were incontrovertibly positive. "I ended up having much greater respect from my husband and children as well as my manager at work," she said. "What is ironic is that I had sold the shares mostly because I wanted their approval. In my mind, I was risking this approval with each one of them by taking back the 'voting rights.' Now I have ended up not only with my shares back, but with much more respect than I had before. Besides this, there is much less confusion in my decision making. I only have to answer to me. Certainly, I take the others into account and actually can do a better job of this knowing that I am doing it out of the best interests of my company. After all, the principal product that I have declared this corporation to be producing is love!" She sounded considerably freer, less burdened, and more enthusiastic about her life.

Summary: Thinking like a CEO—All STOPs are for the purpose of promoting conscious thought and action. They remind us that we are CEOs of our own corporations and encourage us to think

---

CEO EXERCISE WORKSHEET

In making an analogy between a corporation and an individual's human body, you are the CEO of a corporation with amazing inner resources. As such, you are the sole decision maker for the mission, products/services, policies, values, and priorities of this corporation. Here are some questions to consider. When did you last review these factors under your control? Do you still control all of the shares of this corporation? If not, what will it take to buy them back? What is on your agenda for your next board meeting?

What is your **Mission Statement**? _____

_____

What is your **primary Product**? _____

What are your **Policies and Values**? _____

_____

_____

What are your **Priorities**? _____

_____

_____

List your corporation's **Inner Resources:**	**Ownership**		
	% of shares held by others _____%		
	What were the shares sold for?	**Holder**	**% Held**

Date _____ and **Agenda** of the next **Board Meeting:**

from that executive point of view. STOPs enable us to regain mobility when we have lost it. To the extent that a person genuinely recognizes that he is a CEO, it becomes easier to view others as equals and give them the respect due to other sovereign entities. Be alert to those who want shares in your company for little or nothing in return. Be alert to the urge to compensate for lost shares by making an effort to gain a controlling interest in someone else's company. Free people make agreements for mutual interest; they don't sell themselves. Free people have no need to criticize or dominate other sovereign entities. They only have a need to protect and preserve their own inherent freedom and mobility.

The starting place and first foundation of the Inner Game of work is "learning to learn." The second foundation is "thinking for oneself." The capacity for learning and growth without the capacity for independent thinking is of questionable value. Together, these foundations support the mobility to achieve one's goals while knowing that they are truly one's own.

9

COACHING

Coaching is an art that must be learned mostly from experience. In the Inner Game approach, coaching can be defined as the facilitation of mobility. It is the art of creating an environment, through conversation and a way of being, that facilitates the process by which a person can move toward desired goals in a fulfilling manner. It requires one essential ingredient that cannot be taught: caring not only for external results but for the person being coached.

The Inner Game was born in the context of coaching, yet it is all about learning. The two go hand in hand. The coach facilitates learning. The role and practices of the coach were first established in the world of sports and have been proven indispensable in getting the best performance out of individuals and teams. Naturally, managers who appreciate the high levels of individual and team performance among athletes want to emulate what coaching provides.

The coach is not the problem solver. In sports, I had to learn how to teach less, so that more could be learned. The same holds true for a coach in business.

Who Owns the Problem?

One of the first exercises I give in coaching seminars for managers addresses this question. Breaking into threes, one manager would play the role of coach, one would play the client, and one would observe the dialogue. The client would be asked to think of some issue, skill, or goal he would like coaching on. The coach would receive no instructions on how to coach. The observer was given a specific variable to observe and report on.

During the first few minutes of the conversation, the person being coached—the client—would be very animated, working hard to present the relevant information about the problem to the coach. The coach would be in the listening mode. Then, at a certain point, an abrupt change in the body posture of the two people would occur. The client would lean back as if relieved of his problem and the coach would start doing the talking, usually working very hard to come up with ideas or solutions to the problem. Typically, the client would let the coach do the work with occasional interjections aimed at showing why the solution being proposed would not work.

The third person had simply been asked to notice when and if the "ownership of the problem" shifted from one person to another. In almost all cases their feedback confirmed that after a few minutes the client had succeeded in handing off the problem to the coach, who had accepted the lion's share of the burden of solving it.

Most of us learned this pattern of problem solving at a very young age. Probably our parents, eager to be "good parents," solved some of the problems that should have been left to us to solve so that we could gain skill and confidence. We come to expect this kind of help from the coach or parent. We may get an answer, but we don't develop the skill or self-confidence to cope with similar problems in the future. In turn, we tend to try to validate ourselves as parents and coaches by solving the problems of our children or clients.

I learned this lesson twice with my daughter, Stephanie. The first time was when she was in the eighth grade and came to me for help with an algebra problem. She opened with the statement, "I don't get how to do this kind of problem," throwing her book on the dining room table.

"What don't you understand?" I asked.

"I don't understand anything," she replied, clearly signaling that she was expecting me to do the problem for her.

It was one of those problems about how far a boat can travel in a river in a certain amount of time. Quelling the part of me that wanted to see if I could still do algebra, the coach in me took another approach.

"You must have recognized something about this problem to know that it was the kind you didn't understand."

"Yeah, it's one of those rate problems we studied. But I couldn't follow the teacher when she explained it. There's some kind of formula that you're supposed to use, but I can't remember what it is."

"Do you remember anything about it?"

"Yeah, it's really small."

"How small?"

"Oh, I think it's real small. It only has three letters in it. I think it's got a d for distance and something for speed of the boat and then t for time, but I don't know the right order of the three things in the equation."

She was already beginning to sound smart to herself. But she really didn't remember the order, nor did she have the understanding to figure it out. She was getting impatient. I did understand the problem and wanted to help, but I delayed still further.

"You knew one other thing," I said. "You knew that I might know how to solve the problem. And I will explain it to you on one condition. What if I weren't here? Then what would you do? If you can give me three other places you could find out how to do this problem, then I will show you." I knew this was a little painful for her and she thought I was being mean.

"Well, I could always call Susan or Teddy. They're brains. So that's two. I guess as a last resort I could always try reading Chapter Seven in the book. I know it's in there somewhere. So that's three!"

Several things were accomplished. Stephanie got her problem solved. In the process, she recognized that she knew a lot more than she thought she did and felt capable of finding out what she didn't know. I might have spent more time with the conversation than if I had just done the problem for her, but I had saved myself many future hours doing algebra problems. From then on, when she approached me for help, she would say, "Okay, here's what I know and here's what I don't know and here's where I could find out. But you're here and I'd like your help." I usually felt good about accepting such an invitation.

Such simple lessons usually need to be learned more than once, by both sides. Ten years later, Stephanie was having trouble with her first job away from home. She was studying to take the real estate exam in Phoenix and working evenings as a hostess and waitress in a restaurant. She called in tears saying that she was going to have to quit because she couldn't cope with all the things that were being expected of her on the job. She was also beginning to express doubts that she could pass her exam.

Of course, this set off a major alarm in my head. I didn't want her to quit and be out of a job. My parental hat was on, not my coaching hat. I listened to her describe her problem, which she made sound totally insurmountable. She described about five different tasks that she was having trouble with, including using the cash register and an adding machine, and telling the difference between the lemon and the custard pies when they both had the same whipped-cream topping. The demands for all of these tasks would often occur simultaneously, and she would get overwhelmed.

"But I am a professional; I ought to be able to handle this," I thought, and immediately started generating possible solutions in my head. As I started making each brilliant suggestion, she came up with an equally brilliant reason why it wouldn't work. She seemed as determined not to find answers as I was to offer them. The contest went on for some time, neither of us giving an inch, until finally we both grew tired and were ready for bed.

I was very discouraged as I hung up. As father or coach I had been unable to help her. Thoughts of how I could have done things differently kept me awake for hours. Finally, on the verge of giving up, a simple and obvious thought came to me like a revelation. "This isn't my problem. It's her problem." I could hear Self 1 telling me that that was a cruel way to think. "After all, she's your daughter and you are supposed to help." But I stopped thinking about it, relaxed, and finally went to sleep.

The next morning, I woke up thinking more like a coach. I knew that she could handle her problem and she just needed to know that I believed in her (without my telling her, of course). I called her and asked her to rate her present level of skill on each of her five tasks on a scale of one to ten, using seven as the level satisfactory to her boss. Her answers were three on the cash register, four on the adding machine, five on the pies, and seven and seven on the remaining tasks.

"Can you think of what it would take for you to bring the four on the adding machine to a seven or better?"

"Well, there is a spare machine at the restaurant. If I could get permission to take it home . . . and if I could get one of the other waitresses to help me with it . . . I guess maybe in a week's time I could bring it to a seven."

She went through each of the other tasks in a similar manner. I would say little but "What about the pies?" or "How long would that take?" or "Do you feel comfortable that would work?" In fact, I said so little during the entire conversation that she knew she was doing all the work, and when we said our good-byes, she didn't even say "Thanks." I took that as a welcome sign that a good piece of coaching had taken place. I didn't hear from her again for a few weeks, when she called to tell me she had passed her exam and was quitting the restaurant to take an opening position with a real estate firm.

Although this seems a very simple example and certainly did not involve any sophisticated coaching, it points to the huge difference it makes when the person with the problem owns it and is made to feel capable and resourceful in finding his or her own solutions. Sometimes the difference between being stuck and finding one's mobility is as simple as that change in point of view, which, as Alan Kay puts it, is worth at least eighty IQ points. If the coach can be instrumental in that change in point of view, a lot has been accomplished.

Helping the client find the mobility to move toward desired outcomes is then neither problem solving nor simply giving remedial feedback. Neither is it consulting—the giving of expert advice. In sports, the coach is not on the playing field with the players. He can't throw the football. He does his job from the sidelines. The result of his coaching is that the team performs and learns up to the fullest possible potential. It's about letting the team succeed and have the confidence they can succeed in the future.

Coaching as "Eavesdropping" on Someone's Thinking Process—Once you realize that it's not the job of the coach to solve the problem, the question commonly arises, "Well, what is my job—is it just to listen?" Yes, for the most part the job of the coach is to listen well, but there's more to it. Effective coaching in the workplace holds a mirror up for clients, so they can see their own *thinking process*. As a coach, I am not listening for the content of what is being said as much as I am listening to the *way* they are thinking, including how their attention is focused and how they define the key elements of the situation. For example, the question "What do you consider will be the consequences of the proposed action or decision?" is not about content, but it can make a significant difference in how one thinks.

Often when I am coaching, I let the client know from the outset that my role is not to give advice or counsel and that therefore I don't need any detailed background information of the problem at hand. I simply ask the person to start thinking *out loud* about the problem and to allow me to "eavesdrop" on their thought process. I will ask questions or make comments intended to help the person clarify or advance their thinking. This relieves the client of the burden of briefing the coach on the complete picture, and more important, it does not invite a shifting of the responsibility for solving the problem to the coach. The client just starts thinking aloud, and the coach's job is to help the person gain mobility toward his or her desired outcome. Once this understanding is in place between client and coach, the conversation for mobility can usually be completed in a fraction of the time it takes using the traditional model of coach as problem solver.

Transposing—A Primary Coaching Tool

In the many seminars I give to corporate managers on coaching, I normally begin with another simple but profound tool introduced to me by EF. The tool is an aid to communication in general. It is based on the premise that in any communication, what the person hears is more important than what the speaker says and that there is usually a big difference between the two. The better the speaker can anticipate how the listener is apt to hear the message, the more possible it is to get the intended message across.

I introduce the transposing tool to managers with the following exercise: "Call to mind a person you believe could benefit by some coaching from you. This can be someone who reports to you, or a family member or friend.

"Imagine that the person has just received your request to have a coaching session and is wondering what is going to happen.

"Put yourself in the person's shoes and ask yourself the following questions: 'What am I thinking? What am I feeling? What do I want?' "

Most managers conclude that their would-be "coachees" are having similar thoughts: "I am thinking . . . 'I wonder what I did wrong . . . what his problem is.' I am feeling . . . anxious, defensive, angry, embarrassed. I want . . . to make the meeting as short as possible and get out with as much of my self-respect as possible."

Then I ask, "And after the person starts thinking about what mistakes or shortcomings might be the object of the coaching session, what will he start thinking next?"

There is general agreement. There will be excuses, alibis, or blame shifting.

The transposing exercise reveals two things. First, if the prevailing cultural conversation about coaching has to do with getting help with something you've done wrong, the client's internal conversation will be filled with enough fear of judgment and creative defensiveness to make mobility almost impossible. The coach would have to be a genius to be effective with such an inner dialogue going on. Second, transposing works. It becomes obvious to everyone that before throwing around the word *coaching* too liberally in the business environment, it might be a good idea to redefine it. Most athletes actively seek out coaching, while most people in business try to avoid it. You can show other people by your example that you are using the word *coaching* in a very different way.

The ability to transpose another person or team is perhaps the fundamental skill of the coach. It does not necessarily mean that you agree with the other person's point of view, but you learn as much as possible about how he might be thinking and feeling. It is similar to the adage of not judging a person until having walked a mile in his moccasins.

The Inner Game really grew out of my effort to transpose my tennis students before I ever knew there was such a tool. The key question I asked was "What is the player thinking as the ball is coming?" As I tried to imagine this, I became aware that there was a lot of thinking and feeling getting in the way of seeing the ball clearly and hitting it well. It sounded something like this: "I'm thinking . . . 'Uh-oh, here comes a hard one . . . I've got to get into position . . . get my racket back early . . . I'll put it cross-court . . . keep it high over the net . . . make sure I step into the ball with my weight forward. . . . That wind is blowing pretty strong. . . . Last time I missed a shot like this, Coach said I should meet the ball early and follow through. . . . If I can hit a winner, I'll have the game. . . . Wow, there's a lot more topspin on this ball than I thought . . . better step back . . .'

"I'm feeling . . . apprehensive and uncertain . . . I doubt that I'm really going to pull it off, that I can remember everything I have to do. . . . I hope I might make the shot and fear that I won't . . . I am afraid of losing the game and the match . . . I'm determined to do everything 'right.'

"I want . . . to do my best . . . to win . . . to hit a good shot . . . to beat my opponent . . . to do it right . . . to prove myself to others and to myself . . . not to make a fool of myself . . . to look good . . . to have a good story to tell . . . to feel like I did when I hit that last clean winner . . . to avoid repeating the error I made last time I had a shot like this . . . to please my coach."

I also realized that my instructions and critiques of the student were contributing to the self-doubt and self-criticism already ringing in his ear as the ball approached. I was hardly creating a conducive environment for one's best performance.

It was in transposing the students' inner dialogues at the same time as I observed their behaviors and strokes that I realized I had to change the way I coached. The result was that I learned to coach without judgments and virtually without technical instructions. The proof that my transposing was helping my communication with students was evident not only in the speed with which the learning happened but in the ease and enjoyment of the process.

Using the transposing tool allows the coach to have a richer picture of the three primary levels of the other person: thinking, feeling, and will. It is important, however, to remember that at best you are making educated guesses about how the other person thinks and feels. It is important to keep yourself open to feedback and new information, and to be willing to adjust your picture of the other person's reality. The purpose of transposing is not just to gain insight, but to be more effective in your communication. I find it helps me to anticipate how my message might be misinterpreted and to say it in a way that has a better chance of getting through.

Transposing works in most relationships and the advantage goes both ways:

Parent ↔ child
Wife ↔ husband
Teacher ↔ student
Salesperson ↔ customer
Manager ↔ boss
Manager ↔ subordinate
Team player ↔ team player
Opponent ↔ opponent
Competitor ↔ competitor
Friend ↔ friend
Doctor ↔ patient
Negotiator ↔ negotiator
Lecturer ↔ audience
Writer ↔ reader

Using Transposing to Reveal the Underlying Problem—The marketing team in one division of Coca-Cola designed a new marketing strategy and presented it to their national team of account executives. It amounted to a major change in the selling of their set of products and services. As usual, they spent a good deal of money, time, and effort in making a very upbeat presentation. The event was declared a great success because the new plan had been "bought into" by the account executives without much resistance.

However, three months later, when they were reviewing the results of the new plan, they were shocked to see that, with few exceptions, the account executives were not following it. They gave various reasons for this and alluded to plans for implementing the new strategy sometime in the future. Yet every account execu- tive had told the marketing team that the strategy made sense and they could understand the logic of it. The marketing team felt frustrated. They wanted to report to their superiors that their new plan was being successfully implemented.

I was called in for some coaching. They described their situation in a few sentences. "The account executives had totally bought into the plan and now are not acting on it, and we really don't know why. When we ask, they say they believe in the plan and will be implementing it shortly. We don't know what to do short of a typical 'enforcement program,' which will cost us a lot in terms of money, time, and feelings."

They probably wanted a solution from me, but I had none. I asked the marketing team one question: "Have you transposed the account executives?" They knew of the tool, but hadn't used it. They did their transposing first individually, taking notes, and then shared with the team. At the first level, they were all in agreement with "What am I thinking?" They all believed that the account executives had bought into the plan's strategy. They were looking at me as if they weren't getting anywhere.

They took the next step: "What am I feeling?" Again there was general agreement, but this time accompanied by a big "ah-ha." The gist was "I am feeling afraid to try something new . . . I'm afraid it will threaten all the old relationships and loyalties I have built up over the years . . . I'm afraid I don't have the competence to meet my numbers this way." The marketing managers were truly shocked that they had not seen this. I encouraged them to keep going on the feeling level and focus on how the account executives were feeling about the marketing team. The answer was unanimous: "We're afraid to tell them that we're afraid."

When I asked them to complete the transposing with "What do I want?" the answer was again quite homogeneous. "We want to continue with the old way of doing things and keep the marketing guys thinking that we agree with their program and that we are making preparations to implement it."

"So how do you now see the problem?" I asked.

"We have two problems. The first is how to help the accounts feel more confident that they can succeed with the new plan. The second is how to change the current environment so that the account executives feel safe enough to tell us what they are feeling" was the answer. They agreed that the second problem was more difficult but was more important in the long run and could save them many mistakes and much wasted energy in the future.

They solved the first problem themselves in about five minutes. It was not hard once they recognized it. The fact that the second problem was even acknowledged was a huge step forward in that particular culture, where no one ever admitted to feelings of incompetence. The entire session took less than half an hour and resulted in moving in a very different direction. Instead of facing the task of "enforced compliance," the marketing team embarked on a process of removing obstacles to communication between the different levels in the marketing department.

As is often the case in this kind of coaching, the coach had said very little, while the team had done a lot in a short time. The result was improved mobility.

Coaching as a Conversation for Mobility

It is essential to the Inner Game of coaching that the coach try to see from the point of view of the person being coached. By learning to listen to the client nonjudgmentally, the coach learns the most important elements of the craft. Learning to ask questions that help clients reveal more and more to themselves is a natural outcome of such listening. The coach's questions are geared to finding out information not for the purpose of recommending solutions, but for the purpose of helping clients think for themselves and find their own solutions. Ideally, the end result of every coaching conversation is that the client leaves feeling more capable of mobility.

Inner Game coaching can be divided into three conversations: a conversation for awareness (getting the clearest possible picture of current reality), a conversation for choice (getting the clearest possible picture of the desired future outcome), and a conversation for trust (in which the client gains greater access to internal and external resources in order to move from current reality to the desired future). These principles, awareness, choice, and trust are the same ones that provide the foundation for learning itself as well as for focus of attention. In the course of any conversation, awareness, choice, and trust are all present, though one may be emphasized over the others.

The Conversation for Awareness—The purpose of this conversation is to help the person or team being coached (the client) increase awareness of what is—i.e., the important aspects of the current reality. The coach listens both for what stands out to the client as he views the current situation and for what is not standing out. Using questions or statements that focus the attention of the client, the coach can make current reality become more distinct and clear. It is like turning on the headlights of a vehicle and cleaning the windshield. Remember, awareness itself is curative. The primary tool is focus of attention on the critical variables.

The coach can start with a very broad question, such as "What's happening?" and then narrow the domain of observation. "What are you observing about the customer while you are presenting the benefits of your product/service?" "Did you observe anything in particular from the expression on his face or from his body language?" "How did you know when he was receptive to what you were saying or when you were hitting some resistance?" "What is your reaction and action when you notice that resistance?" These questions must be asked in a context of nonjudgment, or they will provoke defensiveness, not increase awareness. Awareness questions do not require answers to be effective. The clients express their awareness as it is. The degree of awareness indicates whether more attention should be paid to that variable or not. As a result of this conversation, both the client and the coach become more aware of the awareness of the client. The seed of each question is usually embedded in the previous response. In the process, the client automatically becomes more conscious about how to direct attention in the next experience. As in all coaching conversations, the point is simply that both client and coach become more conscious and more mobile.

Some open-ended questions for the early stages of the conversation for awareness are listed below:

- What's happening?
- What stands out?
- What do you notice when you look at x?
- How do you feel about this situation?
- What do you understand about x? What don't you understand?
- How would you frame the underlying problem?
- How would you define the task?
- What are the critical variables in this situation?
- How do they relate to one another?
- What are the anticipated consequences of x?
- What standards and time frame have you accepted in this task?
- What has been working? Not working?

The Conversation for Choice—The primary purpose of this conversation is to remind the clients that they are mobile—that they have the capability of choice and can move in the direction of their desired ends. If the conversation for awareness starts with the basic question "What's happening?," then the conversation for choice asks the fundamental question "What do you want?" Awareness is about the present; choice is about the desired future state.

The coach is committed to helping the client find his true commitment. Sometimes this means believing in a level of accomplishment that is well beyond what the client currently exhibits. Part of the art of coaching is to be able to sense the underlying commitment of the client's Self 2 and not to buy into Self 1's limited concepts of what is possible. However, it is not just a matter of indiscriminately setting the bar ever higher. One can set the bar so high that it becomes an interference to Self 2 rather than a recognition of its true abilities.

The coach asks questions that help the client get as clear as possible a picture of what he wants to do. Questions are asked that require the client to step back and consider the purpose behind his desired goal and not just the goal itself. In this conversation the client generates and compares, considers consequences, and makes commitments. It is also a time for looking at conflicting desires that might have to be resolved before true mobility is obtained.

The following are some of the common opening questions I use in the conversation for choice:

- What do you really want?
- What do you want to achieve?
- What are the benefits of x?
- What would be the costs of not pursuing x?
- What would it look like in y weeks, months, years, from now?
- What don't you like about those ends?
- What would be a fulfilling means of getting there?
- What changes would you like to make?
- What do you feel most strongly about in this situation?
- Who or what are you doing this for?
- How does this fit in with your current priorities?
- Do you have any conflicts about this course of action?
- What would success in this endeavor mean to you?
- What alternative possibilities can you consider?

And one of my most-used questions to myself or a client:

- Why would you want to do that?

I find the conversation for choice is most useful in separating the Self 2 desires of the client from the various Self 1 "agendas of the others in us." This enables clients to make choices to move in sync with their own purposes and therefore have a chance of achieving true mobility. The word *commitment* is often defined by clients as obligation—a commitment to others that is not connected to their commitment to themselves. True mobility can be achieved only when a person's commitment to others is in fact connected to and derived from his primary commitment to himself. This is especially difficult for people working in a corporate environment. But when the client can find this kind of alignment of purpose, there is a harmony of motivation that can provide the fuel and clarity to overcome great obstacles in the pursuit of great challenge.

Conversation for Trust—Perhaps the most important outcome of any coaching conversation is that the client ends up feeling respected, valuable, and capable of moving forward. It is a basic trust in oneself and one's potential that gives a person the belief that he can attain mobility. The client feels resourceful, i.e., able to access both the inner and outer resources necessary to reach the goal. The coach does not undermine the confidence of the client by inappropriately being the answer giver, the problem solver, or the judge.

Continuing with the image of a car to represent mobility, *awareness* is like the headlights that enable vision, *choice* is the steering wheel, and *desire* is the fuel. The client, as the driver, has all the inner resources of a human being—including the ability to learn and trust, the key to accessing those resources.

Since trust in oneself is a natural attribute of all children, the job of the coach is to help the client *unlearn* the doubts, fears, and limiting assumptions that inevitably accumulate over time. Trust is perhaps the most delicate of the coaching conversations, and the most critical to the Inner Game. This is the conversation where self-interference is minimized and recognition and confidence in one's capabilities is enhanced.

The Conversation for Trust Calls for *Unlearning* of One's Inner Obstacles—I believe the conversation for trust can best be held by a coach who has become familiar with his own inner obstacles and has made some progress in overcoming them. I never thought Babe Ruth, for example, would have been a good baseball coach. He might just say, "When you see the ball coming at you, swing your hardest and hit the ball over the fence. That's what I do." Natural ability is one thing. Experience overcoming the doubts and fears of the mind that prevent access to one's abilities is another.

It is in creating an environment that minimizes interference with potential that the uniqueness of the Inner Game coach comes forth. Often, it is what is *not* said, rather than what is said, that creates this environment. It is in not judging, not overinstructing, not overcontrolling, that clients realize that their own hands are on the steering wheel and that they may have more capacity and intelligence than their Self 1's had let them realize.

There is no cookie-cutter way of learning this skill as a coach. It is the natural consequence of facing one's own inner obstacles and then learning to put oneself in the shoes of the client. Perhaps the greatest benefit the Inner Game coach brings to the conversation is to trust clients more than the clients trust themselves. And having that trust in the client can be achieved only by having learned an increasingly profound trust in oneself. I know that in my case, my trust in myself was seriously undermined by many factors in my upbringing that taught me to believe in almost everything else but myself. It was only because I was fortunate enough to run into some really good coaches, including EF, that I was able to gradually recognize the imperative of trusting what I now call Self 2. Although most of my coaches didn't call themselves coaches, the best had this one thing in common—they made me believe in myself, in my value, and in my capabilities—especially the capability to learn.

Below are a few questions that can be helpful in the coach's conversation for trust:

- If you could do it any way you wanted, how would you go about accomplishing this task?
- When have you succeeded in a challenge similar to this one?
- At your best, what qualities, attributes, capabilities, do you bring to the situation?

- Direct acknowledgment by the coach of some of the above.
- Where could you find the help you need to accomplish this task?
- What's the most difficult aspect of this task?
- What is your understanding of this situation?
- What first steps do you see?
- How comfortable (confident) do you feel about doing x?
- What would it take to make you feel more comfortable?
- What did you like most about the way you accomplished this task?

One of the biggest problems in the modern corporate environment is the breakdown of trust in the individual. When one can't trust oneself or one's environment, it is not easy to recognize one's true capabilities or current limitations. Instead, people end up accepting tasks that are often beyond the capabilities of the individual or team without anyone feeling confident enough to say so. How many times in the corporate environment do you expect that you will hear someone saying, "I believe that that is beyond my present capabilities," or simply, "I don't know how to do that"? Yet only by being able to assess one's competencies accurately, without either Self 1's doubt or its inflated bravado, can one expand capability. The acceptance of tasks or standards that are out of one's reach sows self-doubt just as failing to accept challenges that require stretching and learning confirms self-doubt. In the conversation for trust, the coach provides the safety and encouragement that helps the client find the appropriate level of challenge to accept.

Coaching Mobility: A Synthesis of the Three Conversations—By using these three conversations, the Inner Game coach helps the client gain mobility. He helps a stuck client get unstuck, and circumvent both inner and outer obstacles. Whether the client is an individual or a team, the coach keeps the client focused on both the outer and the Inner Game goals, helping provide a constant synthesis and balance between the two. The outside job gets done and the person doing it enjoys and learns in the process. At all times, the client's hands are on the steering wheel. The client remains the driver of his own vehicle, while the mobility coach remains the passenger.

The three conversations are not necessarily conducted in any particular order. Elements of each are contained in the other. Usually, I find that an extended coaching conversation will cycle through each conversation many times at different levels. What is consistent is the environment of nonjudgment, trust, and purpose. Within that environment, there is room for creative and unexpected movement toward the chosen goal. Both client and coach can learn a great deal from the coaching conversation.

The coach brings to all these conversations a point of view that is hopefully not as caught up in the performance momentum as is that of the client. Because the coach is not "on the team" operationally, it is often easier to establish a stepped-back perspective. Standing outside the assumptions and demands of the performance momentum, the coach can help the client to STOP: *step back, think,* and *organize* before *proceeding.*

Functions of an Inner Game Coach

No description of the functions of a coach can replace learning from experience. The following, however, is a partial list of functions of an Inner Game coach that may serve to clarify the direction of the coach or provide critical variables for the coaching process.

The Inner Game coach helps clients:

- Identify beneficial learning goals.
- Identify critical variables to assist with focus.
- Keep learning, experience, and performance goals in balance.
- Grant themselves mobility.

- Remain in the CEO's chair and retain all their shares.
- Recognize outmoded assumptions and definitions.
- Keep task and purpose in sync.
- Be more aware of both time and task completion.
- Keep in touch with feeling, intuition, and creativity.
- Develop people skills—balance team and task integrity.
- Improve skills.
- Access inner and outer resources.
- Keep workload, ability, and time in sync.
- Identify and overcome blocks to mobility.

The Inner Game coach:

- Encourages acceptance of mobility.
- Fosters a nonjudgmental environment.
- Provides learning/coaching tools as appropriate.
- Provides another perspective and source of insight as needed.

A Toolbox for the Inner Game Coach

All the tools and concepts in this book are as applicable to coaching as they are to learning. I like to think of this next section as a starting toolbox for the coach. It contains some tools we've already discussed (in which case I've provided a page reference) as well as some new information on control and feedback.

·Focus on Critical Variables—This is a principal tool (see pages 62–77) for the awareness conversation. It accomplishes two things at once—reducing Self 1 interference and giving useful feedback for performance and learning.

Critical variables can be identified for any situation or activity. It is best to limit the number of variables to seven. A maximum of seven more specific subvariables can be identified for each general variable. This enables the focus to be as broad or as narrow as appropriate to the desired goals. Using an example from tennis, the movement of the tennis ball could be considered a general variable, with speed, trajectory, direction, spin, and height as the subvariables. Likewise, the general variable of "customer need" can be broken down into more specific subvariables, such as customer perception of benefits, urgency, affordability, and offerings of competition.

A variable is not an instruction to do something. It is a focus for attention. The coach listens to the client talk about a given situation or activity and notices what is and is not being paid attention to. By answering questions such as "What do you notice as you look at x or consider y?," coach and client become more attuned to the contents of the client's awareness. This allows both to focus attention to bring about greater clarity and learning.

• STOP—All coaching could be considered a use of the STOP tool (see pages 144–164). Coaching generally occurs before an upcoming task or project (the setup conversation), during a pause in the action of the task, or afterward (the debriefing). During a STOP, coach and client have the time to set goals, identify critical variables, and transpose, in order to maximize the learning from the upcoming work experience. After the given work experience, a debriefing can be held to help assimilate and maximize the benefits of the learning.

• Transposing—The coach not only can transpose clients (see pages 183–188), but can increase the clients' awareness of key people with whom they interact by having the clients transpose them. Many of the interteam or interpersonal conflicts that I have seen interfere with work can be resolved as team members learn to use the transposing tool. Once the clients are familiar with the tool, the coach can simply employ a simple request, "Have you transposed Bob, Mary, the customer, the end user?" Coaching the transposition so that it has sufficient depth and richness comes with the experience of using the tool.

· **The Control Questions**—There are three questions that I find indispensable as a coach. All three address the issue of control. They help the client focus on what is controllable and let go of what is not. I don't always use them in the simple form given below, but they are usually embedded in any coaching conversations, especially the conversation for trust. The questions should be asked in this order:

- What don't you control here?
- What have you been trying to control?
- What could you control that you have not?

The first question gives a person the chance to recognize that there are probably many variables in a situation that he does not control. Take an example of any business conversation between A and B where A is trying to "make a point" or "sell an idea" or convince B of the wisdom of a certain course of action. B could be a boss, a customer, or a co-worker. A might think that he is quite smart and skilled at presenting his case. But how many of the factors for success does A actually control?

Here's a partial list:

- A does not control B's attitude or receptivity to the idea.
- A does not control how well B will listen to A.
- A does not control B's motivation, needs, or priorities.
- A does not control B's time availability.
- A does not control whether B likes A.
- A does not control B's ability to understand A's point.
- A does not control how B is going to interpret A's communication.
- A does not control whether B accepts A's point in the end.

A may try logic, facts, or fancy show-and-tell techniques. B may either comply, setting up a future "buyer's remorse" situation, or determine not to be talked into anything.

A could get angry and demand an answer.
B could get stubborn and say no.
What are some of the factors that A *could* control?

- His attitude toward B.
- His attitude toward learning.
- How receptively he listens to B.
- His acknowledgment of B's points.
- His use of aggressiveness.
- His respect for B's choice to accept or decline.
- His homework regarding B's needs, values, desires; transposing B.
- His respect for B's time.
- His own expression of enthusiasm for his idea.
- The amount of time spent speaking versus listening.

Obviously, each of these factors that A does not control is an important factor in how B responds to A's communication. A begins to realize that there is a lot that he simply is not in control of. This can be a humbling reality check for A.

Here is a list of some of the things that A was trying to control:

- A asked B for the appointment and indicated the amount of time needed.
- A gave B a general idea of the subject matter beforehand.
- A carefully outlined his arguments and the benefits to B.
- A did his homework to gain background knowledge and information.
- A had decided that he would be as aggressive as necessary to gain acceptance.

Each of these factors could help A succeed, but obviously could not guarantee success. In his desire to control the outcome, A might also try to control some of the factors that he doesn't have control over and in so doing will probably work against his success. For example:

- A, not getting immediate acceptance, might try to "force" agreement.
- B feels the pressure, starts to resist, looks for reasons for not accepting.

A's assertive management of the variables that are in his control will not guarantee that B will accept the idea, but might heighten the probability and contribute something positive to A's ongoing relationship with B.

In sports as well as in business, I have found that much of the resistance to change comes from trying to overcontrol. A golfer tries too hard to control the flight of the ball and his muscles overtighten and cause a loss in control. This is like a manager who tries to overcontrol his subordinates. They "overtighten" and resist taking responsibility. The result is a lack of real control over desired outcomes. True responsibility is a matter of choice and cannot be controlled; it has to be taken willingly.

Feedback—Feedback is often considered the primary tool of the coach. What is usually meant by feedback is "evaluation of performance." Although this function can be beneficial, it makes the coaching relationship vulnerable to becoming judgmental. There are two other kinds of feedback that are useful and that are not part of the traditional concept of performance evaluation.

The first is feedback as a mirror. The point is for the client to become more self-aware. The coaching questions allow the student to get increased feedback from his direct experience of both the action and its results. For example, "What were the consequences of x?" "How did you feel about y?" "What are your priorities here?" "How much time did z take?" "How much has this project cost to date?" "What has been accomplished thus far?" None of these questions imply a right or wrong answer. They invite the client to become more aware of what is.

The second kind of nonevaluative feedback is that in which the coach says what he notices. If the player says, "I think my weight was mostly on my front foot when I made contact with the ball," the coach might say, "It looked to me like it was mostly on your back foot. Why don't you hit another and check it out?" There is no judgment of the rightness or the wrongness, just a report of what was observed by the coach. Likewise, a coach can share perceptions and insights about any work situation for the sole purpose of increasing awareness or provoking thought on the part of the client without being evaluative. However, many people have a difficult time hearing an observation from another person without assuming that there is an evaluation embedded in it. Knowing this, the coach can make the necessary effort to communicate that no judgment or evaluation is intended.

Finally, evaluative feedback can be useful to the client in some cases, if it's done with care and is grounded in fact. This is especially true when the client is having difficulty making a clear or accurate self-evaluation. When giving evaluative feedback, the coach should exercise extra caution to limit the evaluation to the performance and avoid the possible perception of judging the person. Again the coach must be aware that the client's Self 1 may just be waiting for the chance to turn an evaluation of performance into an evaluation of self. When this is allowed to happen, any benefit from the feedback about performance is liable to be lost by the damage done by negative self-evaluation.

When evaluative feedback is called for, it should obey some common ground rules. It should be

- Directed toward the deed, not the doer.
- Grounded in observation of fact.
- Made against previously agreed-upon standards.
- Made by a person competent to make the assessment.
- Made in the interest of heightened mobility, i.e., improved clarity or future action.

Self-Coaching

I am often asked the question, "Is it possible to coach yourself?" On the one hand, the answer is no. The advantage of a coach is that he is offering a different set of eyes and a different perspective, in some cases holding up a mirror. The value of coaching lies precisely in the fact that the coach is *not* you and can see things differently. Otherwise, the coach would clearly be redundant.

On the other hand, the answer is yes. If coaching is creating an environment in which a person learns and performs, then we are all doing that for ourselves all the time. Unfortunately, our Self 1's are usually the ones creating the environment in which we perform and that is not always conducive to being our best. One of the advantages of external coaching is that by listening to a good coach, we can more easily ignore the overly critical and controlling voices of our own Self 1's. One of the primary functions of the coach is to help the client improve the internal dialogue he carries around with him and that influences how he learns and performs when the coach isn't around. So perhaps the best answer to the question is yes. It is ultimately most important that we improve our own capacity for self-coaching. And to that end, periodic good coaching from another can be very helpful.

Executive Coaching as a Self-organizing Initiative—I have seen many corporations try to "roll out" courses on executive coaching, only to find that it took a great deal of effort, time, and money to train coaches, and that there was relatively little responsiveness on the part of those being coached. Failure of these programs can usually be attributed to two factors: (1) the coaches are trained as coaches but not as learners; and (2) the learners aren't shown the benefits of being coached, nor do they accept responsibility for their own growth and development.

Recently, I was asked by Mel Bergstein, CEO of a rapidly growing strategic consulting firm named Diamond Technology Partners, to help design the company's learning strategy. A leader in the application of digital technology to business strategy, this partnership had made a conscious commitment to learning and to the professional development of their consultants as well as their clients. The company wanted all consultants trained in coaching so that they could better develop the capabilities of all their project teams. They also believed that the coaching skills learned would be beneficial in their client work. People who are paid to have answers do not always find it easy to learn the skills that allow the client to come up with his own answers. There is a special challenge in coaching consultants how to coach.

So we took a different approach. After an initial presentation of The Inner Game of Work to the consultants, I asked for volunteers who would be willing to participate in a research project directed toward applying Inner Game principles to consulting practices. Each participant would do "research" on some specific application that was of high interest to him or her personally. The results of their findings would be made available to anyone else in the company who was interested. There was to be no further course work. All the research would be done in the laboratory of the participant's own work experience. The participants would set the goals of their own research, ask their own questions, and come up with their own answers, the practicality of which would be tested in their own experience before being shared with others.

The participants were told that the research would be entirely of their own design. Furthermore, since the learning was to take place from their interaction with their own work experience, the only extra time required after outlining their project goals was to engage in the "learning brief" and "debrief" on either side of a selected work experience (see "The Experience Sandwich," p. 97) Each would have available to them telephone coaching (initially from myself) as well as group coaching conversations once every two weeks until the process became self-generating. After an initial commitment of one hour per week for a month, each participant would be free to leave or continue with the project according to its perceived individual benefit.

The design was very simple and involved little logistical support or expense. Participants would have a firsthand experience of the benefits of this approach to learning, would have the chance to share their discoveries with their colleagues, and without making a conscious effort to do so, would learn the basic skills of coaching. My direct involvement as coach ended as soon as the research became self-generating among the initial participants and they took on the coaching role with new researchers. The growth of the project was spontaneous and involved almost no organizational control.

The first step after volunteering for the project was for each researcher to come up with a research objective. To help with their selection, the following three questions were asked: (1) What are you most interested in right now?; (2) What is your current work experience "trying to teach you"?; and (3) What, if learned, would most benefit you and your colleagues? The next step was to select work activities that would serve as the laboratory for their research and critical variables to use as a focus of their attention.

Here's an example of the kinds of research intially selected by participants:

Researcher 1:

Area of Research: Understanding client need

Research Objective: Gain in ability to think with the client's perspective

Perceived Obstacles: Focus on results at expense of process

Research Experience: Direct client meetings; problem-solving meetings with team

Selected Critical Variables: Client thought process; number and kind of questions I ask

Learning Tools: Transposing; control questions; STOP

Initial Findings: "Following my interest in how others think in ways different from the ways I think, I started asking more and better questions. This produced better answers and a sense of greater collaboration. Meetings were perceived as more interesting and of greater value. I got better results with less stress and found a surprising joy in this kind of learning. I was especially surprised to find that my team members appreciated meetings more because I seemed more interested in their thinking than in just giving them the benefit of mine."

Researcher 2:

Area of Research: Client presentations

Research Objective: How to maintain composure and access to abilities during high-pressure presentations

Perceived Obstacles: Anxiety and self-doubt

Research Experience: High risk: new-client sales presentations; medium risk: project presentations with ongoing client work teams; low risk: nonbusiness presentations on martial arts

Selected Critical Variables: Client interest level/my degree of composure

Learning Tools: Transposing; redefining

Initial Findings: "When I focused more attention on the client, I found myself less self-conscious. My responses were more intuitive, and the client seemed to feel more respected. As a consequence, my confidence grew. Practice in the low- and medium-risk activities eventually allowed me to feel more composed during the high-risk situations. I also learned that I was creating most of the pressure in my own thinking."

Researcher 3:

Area of Research: Multitask planning

Research Objective: How to simplify planning process in complex, highly interdependent tasks

Perceived Obstacles: Perception of too much to do with too little time; maintaining clarity of priorities in highly detailed and complex tasks

Research Experience: Moving through my daily to-do lists

Selected Critical Variables: Self-directed versus other-directed tasks; degree of complexity of planning process; amount of planning committed to paper

Initial Findings: "I was surprised to find that my planning was much more complex in those tasks that I perceived I 'had to do' compared to those that I did because I felt they were important. This led to the exploration of how I unconsciously sabotaged those tasks that I felt somehow coerced into doing. It's raising some very interesting questions about how I select the work I do.

The amount of time I am spending creating written plans is decreasing, and my feeling of accomplishment at getting done what is important is increasing."

At the time of the writing of this book, it is too early to evaluate the long-term benefits of this initiative. But the early results are encouraging and show that it is possible to initiate a grass-roots learning initiative with very little organizational presence or control.

At first most of the researchers experienced some difficulty remembering the learning context. It was a new kind of practice and required self-discipline without the usual organizational incentives. Good intentions notwithstanding, they found that the path of least resistance was to fall into performance momentum. What helped in the initial part of their learning curve was using a research notebook in which they recorded their briefing and debriefing thinking. They also needed the support of regular telephone coaching sessions, which gave them the chance to share difficulties as well as successes. The coach learns to anticipate the swing from high expectations at the outset of any new endeavor to bitter disappointment at seeing the habits and obstacles of the past exert their force.

But once the researchers began to see the benefits of the time spent, and established the new practices as part of their work life, mobility began to be self-evident. They then felt confident to invite others on their teams to participate in the project and began to coach them. This increased the reminders coming from their immediate work environment. It began to be more "normal" to hear conversations among work teams about what they were exploring and finding. The numbers of participants increased, which created a demand for coaching. The initiative spread spontaneously and at its own rate, without the normal resistance met by most organizational change initiatives.

Coaching cannot be done in a vacuum. If the learner doesn't want to learn, it doesn't make any difference if the coach is a great coach. Coaching is a dance in which the learner, not the coach, is the leader. The best way the coach can learn the role is by knowing what it is like to be a learner who experiences the benefits of being coached.

Recently, Bill Blazek, the editor of a business journal called *The Executive Coach,* conducted an interview with me on the subject of Inner Game coaching in business. I've included several excerpts from this interview that highlight some of the aspects of coaching not yet covered and underscore others that bear repeating.

BB: Why, in your opinion, has coaching become such a hot topic in the business and corporate worlds?

TG: Because learning has become more important. In the so-called knowledge age of business, the critical competitive factor is how well and how rapidly you can grow your people.

Therefore, the first and constant task of the coach is to keep the responsibility for learning with the client. In the Inner Game approach to coaching, this means that the client not only is willing to learn from the coach but has accepted personal responsibility for learning from his or her day-to-day experience.

BB: In your view, should managers be coaches?

TG: They should learn to coach. But that does not mean they should abdicate their primary commitment to produce business results through people. A manager/coach learns to wear different hats in different conversations. As a manager, he might tell the team, "Here's what we must accomplish, these are the standards, this is the time line, and these are the available resources." With his coaching hat on, he might say, "Now that you are clear about your performance goals, what are you going to need to learn in order to achieve them?" As coach, the primary commitment is to integrity of teamwork and the development of the skills necessary to accomplish the performance goals. The coach is someone with whom you have to feel safe to disclose your shortcomings, your mistakes, and your personal aspirations. For this reason, in some environments, the coaching and managing functions are performed better if done by different people.

BB: So the manager is responsible for setting clear goals, while the coach helps the employee reach the goals?

TG: Yes. The coach also helps the individual or team make sure that individual, team, and corporate goals are as aligned as possible so there is minimal conflict among the three sets of goals.

BB: What kind of business problems do you see the Inner Game helping with?

TG: Those problems that involve the human dimension. There are more human problems than ever and they are usually solved by managers who are more used to solving the problems of systems and projects. In the past century, workers were molded and folded into business systems and processes. In this century, such a strategy won't work. Business systems must harmonize with the processes of how human beings work best and grow best, not the other way around.

BB: So, by paying more attention to the Inner Game in a corporate setting, the systems—the ways things are organized and the strategies used—will begin to blend with the human factor.

TG: Yes, I believe so. The more business leadership recognizes that people really are their most important resources, the more they will adapt business systems and models to what works for the human being. Managers will have to become more than project managers. They must develop a new level of people skills to be able to cope with workers who find themselves under greater pressure for results yet need to feel safe enough to learn and grow. I find it ironic that heightened competitive demands in the new century are going to require that business mentality become much more of a human mentality. Before, leaders may have been able to succeed without much skill or concern about human vulnerabilities and feelings. Now, they won't succeed without both profound understanding of and the ability to deal with the human factor. Threat of being fired will no longer be sufficient to ensure cooperation. The best workers will be independent thinkers who, if they don't like how they are being treated, will simply find better work environments.

BB: I went to Ohio State during the reign of the great Woody Hayes, and you could plainly see how his players were afraid of him. Vince Lombardi was another with a mince-no-words coaching style. But today there is a broad spectrum of coaching styles between the "hard" and the "soft" approaches. Where does the Inner Game lie on this spectrum?

TG: Style is one thing and substance another. The important thing is that the *care* be there. The coach has to care about the person being coached and the person needs to know it. Then there can be a time for both hard and soft styles. I have been on the receiving end of the mince-no-words approach when it really helped me because I knew I was not being personally attacked. There have also been times when I have needed a more receptive and encouraging approach. So much depends on the situation and the relationship that has been established between coach and student. I don't believe that a good coaching relationship is ever characterized by fear. Fear will generally cause self-interference and lessen one's maximum performance. The relationship should, I believe, be one of mutual respect and trust, one in which the coach has the best interests of the client in mind.

BB: This makes me think of a coach more like John Wooden. He seems to me to have led more by his values than by dominating his players through fear.

TG: I know John Wooden and have talked with him about this. I know he commanded great respect from his players even though he was quite soft-spoken. I also know he could be very direct and put up with no nonsense from his players. I believe he earned a great deal of respect because he was such a student of the game. As a result, he was perceived as embodying the quality of humility and at the same time a genuine authority. This combination provided a coaching environment that produced the best college basketball records ever.

BB: Talking about the hard-versus-soft approach to coaching, there are some people who believe that in order to improve, we have to focus on the negative and stop kidding ourselves. They seem to argue for a tough love approach in the performance area. How do you address this concern?

TG: Well, it's fine to be tough so long as you are sure the love is there. It's really easy for it not to be tough love at all, but tough anger, tough criticism, and tough revenge. As I said, the care and respect of the coach for the student have to be clear. The more obvious they are to the student, the tougher the coach can be. But if you get too tough with someone who doesn't trust you, you will kill the very thing you are trying to activate. You will sow more self-doubt than self-confidence. So the coach who cares has to be wise about when to be tough and when to be nurturing.

BB: One of your ideas that I find most intriguing is that you say that coaching doesn't require expertise in the subject matter. This flies in the face of conventional wisdom. Would you tell us why you think this way?

TG: First, I should say that there is nothing wrong with the coach having expertise in the subject matter so long as it isn't used to make the client feel stupid or keep him from doing his own learning. When you know a lot, it's all too easy to start teaching. But coaching is not so much about telling the client what *you* know as it is about helping him discover what he already knows, or can find out for himself. Teaching takes a long time and is about imparting knowledge. Coaching can be viewed not so much as a process of *adding* as it is a process of *subtracting,* or *unlearning* whatever is getting in the way of movement toward the client's desired goal.

BB: Can you give an example of a coaching conversation where the coach doesn't have expertise?

TG: One example that comes to mind is the time that I gave a presentation on the Inner Game to the Houston Philharmonic Orchestra. After a brief presentation, they wanted a demonstration, and the tuba player volunteered. I play no musical instrument and had never heard a solo tuba. When the tuba player arrived on-stage, I asked him what he would most like to learn.

"What I find most difficult is articulation in the upper range," he said. I had no idea what he was talking about, but asked him to play a passage. It sounded good to me, but he shook his head, obviously not pleased with his performance.

"What did you notice?" I asked, knowing I didn't really have to know anything myself, because I was going to rely on his knowledge.

"It wasn't so clean."

"How did you know?" I asked.

"That's an interesting question. I can't actually hear it when it happens because the bell of the tuba is too far from my ear. But I can feel it in my tongue," he reported, getting me close to the critical variables I needed to use as a focus of attention.

"What happens in your tongue?"

"Well, in difficult passages like this one, with upper-range notes, it often starts feeling dry and a little thick."

I had everything I needed. "Play the same passage again, but this time don't try hard to keep the articulation clean. I merely want you to notice any changes in the degree of moisture in your tongue as you play the passage."

He played the same passage and I could detect no changes. They both sounded good to my untrained ear. But the rest of the orchestra got up out of their seats and gave him a standing ovation! And the tuba player had a satisfied and somewhat surprised smile on his face.

Without showing any particular interest in his results, I asked him what he noticed about his tongue as he played the passage. "It stayed moist the entire time," he said, "and it never felt thick."

"Why do you think that was?" I asked, though I was already formulating an answer in my head.

"I felt more relaxed. The pressure was off when you said don't try hard for clean articulation and I was very curious to notice what was happening with my tongue."

"Maybe when you feel the pressure," I added, "the anxiety dries out your tongue a little and makes it feel thicker. There isn't much pressure when you are focused on what's happening. You just let go of a little fear, and Self 2 knew what to do."

BB: So the coach, without having technical knowledge, can help the client get around whatever is blocking his best performance.

TG: Yes. You don't want to assume clients know more or less than they actually do. You want to be accurate. Define the gap between what is known and what needs to be known. Then paying close attention to experience will usually get rid of the interference, and whatever learning is necessary to close the gap can take place. Maybe the person needs to go to a teacher if there is a knowledge gap. Maybe the gap can be closed by learning from experience. What the coach provides is the nonjudgmental awareness so that the learning can take place in either case.

BB: I can see that coaching conversations like that needn't take very much time.

TG: That's true. If the coach does not play the role of teacher or problem solver, it doesn't take too much time. Once trust is established and both student and coach understand the process, effective coaching can happen in the space of a single question. A short conversation that sets the learning context before a given learning experience and a short debriefing afterward is all that is required. It can be a highly leveraged activity—short on time and long on payoffs.

BB: Talking about time, I would say that sooner or later, every client who wants coaching needs help with time management. How would Inner Game principles apply to that situation?

TG: In the first place, time management is a misnomer. No matter what *we* do, time moves along doing what it does, unaffected by us. We have no choice but to stay in the present. We can't live one moment into the future or relive one moment of the past.

So the best we can do is manage what we *do* with the time we have. Here there are a few critical variables: (1) knowing how long the things you do take you; (2) knowing how much of your time you have already committed, so that you don't commit more than you have; and (3) being aware of how your use of time matches up with your priorities. By simply becoming more aware of these three factors, without judgment, and without pressure to move faster, a person can be helped to make the best use of time. Usually, when I ask people to simply observe these variables, they are surprised at how unaware of time they have been. As the awareness grows more accurate, improvements in efficiency and focus are automatic. Then time can actually be perceived as a friend and not as the enemy.

BB: One last question: How would you recommend a person who wanted to become an executive coach learn this art?

TG: There are three ways to learn coaching. The least important is the theory and training you might receive. You can read about coaching or take a coaching workshop. But the two important ways are from the direct experience of coaching and of being coached. Coach as much as possible and ask for coaching as much as possible. Learn from both what works and what doesn't work. If you don't like being coached, you probably won't be a good coach for others. My clients have taught me the most about coaching— not by telling me how to coach, but by responding as they did to me. I pay attention to these responses as well as to my Self 2 feelings and intuitions.

Regardless of the learning environment, I always cover the three coaching principles of awareness, choice, and trust. Increased mobility on the part of the client follows naturally.

As corporate leaders become more aware of the implications of change on their organizations, they realize that learning must be a core value of their corporate culture. As a result, they look to coaching as the most cost-effective means of developing learning skills in their employees.

10

THE INHERENT AMBITION

This book has been an attempt to look anew at the most basic premises underlying how we work in our culture. It has suggested that when we work, much of the time we are being driven by factors we are not conscious of. The goal has been to learn true mobility, to work consciously, and to be free human beings while working. This last chapter is a discussion of *desire*—the force that fuels all work. Desire is the most personal, most important, and yet most difficult factor to put our fingers on. It is the very heart of our quest.

In the Beginning, There Is Desire

What is the impulse that moves us to purposeful action? What is it that motivates or drives our work? We tend to give more thought to how well we are working, what we are accomplishing, or how to get better results. Seldom do we reflect on what is the generating force behind our work itself—what *fuels* our movement toward our work goals.

Some might think this question is too obvious to be worth asking. Others might think it is too deep to address here. Perhaps it is both. In either case, it is not an easy topic, but I know of no other that is more important. I believe that desire is at the heart of the matter of work, and perhaps of all things human. It is often said that "where there is a will, there is a way." But we spend most of our time trying to understand "the way" and very little time trying to understand the source of "the will."

I confronted the issue of desire one day when I was thinking about the question "What initiates the golf swing?" Some say the hands; some say the shoulders; some say the torso. Then I realized, "No, what initiates the swing is the *desire* to hit the ball. If there were no desire to hit the ball, there would be no swing." A person might ask himself, "Where do I *want* to hit this ball?" Then he might visualize the ball flying through the air and ending up in the middle of the fairway. But where did that vision come from? Was it merely a thought that produced the vision, or was it a *want* that could be felt? This line of inquiry led me to look for the source of desire—whether one is hitting a golf ball or working on a project. It led to the simplest and most important lesson of the Inner Game: *It all begins with desire.*

Reflect on these questions about desire as it relates to working:

- How clear are you about what you want?
- What do you *really* want?
- How connected do you feel to your passion, to the wellspring of your desire?
- Have you ever felt more connected? When, and to what?
- As you look at your different desires, do they seem to be aligned or to be pulling in separate directions?
- Where do your desires come from—thought or feeling?
- How clearly can you distinguish *your* desires from the expectations of other people?
- To what extent do you feel you are "steering" your desires versus being driven by them?
- Do you feel *free* while working?
- What does being free mean to you?

- Do you desire to be free?
- How do you know?

"*What* Do I Want?"—This is one of the most basic and important human questions. "What do I *really* want?" is an even more important question. If the answers to these questions are not clear to you right now, where can you go to find them? Can they be found in a book, through a friend, or by thinking about them? For most difficult questions, we can find an expert who has studied the subject. But who has studied the subject of what *you* want? Are you not the only expert on that? We each have to answer the question of what we want individually and independently. And we have to do our own research.

Where will I go to do this research? Probably, I will go to that great library that sits on top of my neck and I will start *thinking*. Maybe the answers will include "I need to work to earn my living, to pay my bills, to feed myself or my family . . . to support my lifestyle . . . to survive . . . to succeed and be recognized . . . to make a contribution . . . to make a difference . . . to be normal . . . to be a good father, mother, person . . . I am expected to work . . . I have to make something of myself . . . I have obligations and I have responsibilities . . . I work because I have a to-do list a mile long . . . In fact, I have too much work to do to take time to ask myself about what I want."

Many of the "wants" we think of first are actually based on underlying "don't wants." We want a job because we don't want to starve. We want money because we don't want the consequences of not paying our bills. We work hard to make a good impression because we don't want to look foolish or to be looked down upon. I want what others around me want because I don't want to feel uncertain or alone. Perhaps the head is not the best place to look for the answer to the question of what I really want. It's usually filled with conflicting messages. Perhaps there is another place to look.

"*Where* Is My Desire?"—Where does our desire come from? Can we locate the *feeling* that we call desire? Where can we look for the feeling that generates our desire to work? If we could find *where* the feeling was, would it have something to tell us about *what* we really wanted?

In many ways, we are in kindergarten on the subject of desire, even though desire is a factor that motivates every life activity as well as every aspect of work. Discovering our desire may take a little time, a little patience, and even a little soul-searching. So I am asking you to persevere even though it may be new territory. Finding your core desire and ambition can provide your core independence as a worker. It can provide the fuel that makes mobility possible. It can make work a fulfilling experience instead of a frustrating and stressful one.

Felt Desire—At root, is desire a feeling or a thought?

Is it possible to connect consciously with my core desire? Maybe I can't get there by thought alone but must *feel* my way to it. Isn't that the way I did it as a child before I started thinking? I wanted food when I *felt* hungry, drink when I *felt* thirsty, and sleep when I *felt* sleepy. I didn't have to think about those wants to know when I had them or when they were fulfilled.

I am interested in connecting with my *felt* desire in work. I want to gain better and better access to the generator of passion. As I make that declaration, I can't help but notice some anxiety arising. It seems safer to continue working as usual. Why rock the boat? What if I find I have no true desire to work? What if I find I don't really feel any desire for what I have been pursuing all along?

In my dictionary, the word *desire* has a very simple meaning—"strong want or longing." It sounds as if it refers to a feeling more than to a thought. What image is evoked by the word *desire* as you hear it alone? If you were in a bookstore and found a book with the single-word title *Desire,* what would you guess the book was about?

I was surprised to discover how few words in the English language refer to strong desire. Those that do, like *passion, drive,* and *desire* itself, are most usually associated with sexual desire. Such a poverty of language often is a sign of poverty of *meaning*. Our lack of vocabulary reflects a lack of distinctions and contributes to a cultural blind spot.

Is Desire Trustworthy?—I don't know about you, but I was brought up to believe that my wants or desires were less than trustworthy. Ideals were trustworthy. Reason was trustworthy. Desires were suspect. They pulled me away from reason and from "our" ideals. Of course, it was never quite explained where I was supposed to get the *desire* to follow the ideals. The implied motivator, of course, was fear—fear of the consequences of not following the ideals—fear of not being accepted, sometimes fear of "eternal suffering." I imagine that these same fears motivated those who were passing the ideals on to me.

I was taught that whatever I wanted I should surrender it to "God." Do what "God" wants, *not* what you want. That was the safe and true road. Of course, I didn't really know what "God" wanted, but there were always plenty of people more than happy to speak on his behalf. The message was clear: What "God" wanted and I wanted were at different ends of the spectrum. And "God" was very big and I was very small, and he held in his hands the ultimate in rewards and punishments.

At first, I decided that I could get a hint about what "God" wanted by letting it be the opposite of what I wanted. If I wanted to talk, he must want me to be quiet. If I wanted to play, he wanted me to study. If I wanted to sleep, he wanted me to wake, and if I wanted to stay awake, he wanted me to go to sleep. After a while, it didn't make sense to check what I wanted because whatever it was, it wasn't going to be the right thing to do. So I learned to avoid this conflict by doing what was expected of me. To accomplish this end only required thinking and I grew increasingly separated from the feeling of my own desire.

In college, I was introduced to the revered champion of psychology, Dr. Sigmund Freud. He spoke convincingly on the idea of God being little more than a substitute father figure. But unfortunately, Dr. Freud had no more regard for the validity of human desire than the religions that he criticized. I understood him to say that my deepest desires, seated in my "libido," were animal in nature. They wanted mostly to conquer and to have sexual gratification. My desires were highly uncivilized and would be devastating to myself and to others if I allowed them expression without restraint.

The understanding I took away was that desire was still not trustworthy and, though it shouldn't be repressed, it had to be "redirected" toward culturally acceptable ends. According to Dr. Freud, we have some sophisticated mental equipment that keeps us from knowing too directly what that libido really wants in the first place. Then we have another piece of equipment that enables us to alter, or sublimate, those base desires into civilized ones such as creativity and productivity and, of course, civilized "love."

The message was that if it were not for what I learned from society, I would be an untamed beast. But if I am given the right books to read and told the right things by parents, teachers, and the venerable institutions of my society, I can transcend my beastly desires and learn to be a "responsible contributor to society."

As I look back on the cornerstones of my conditioning, I see to my surprise that the atheist Freud and my religious upbringing were fundamentally in agreement. Both assumed that human nature was basically bad and in need of control from outside. Freud told me I needed "civilization" and not religion. Religion told me I needed obedience to the precepts and laws of its "God." Both agreed that my desires would get me into trouble. My religion told me I'm bad, but "God" will save me; Freud said I'm "bad" at the core, but "enculturation" will save me. Bottom line: I shouldn't trust my desire. And if I can't trust my core desire, is it really possible to trust myself? The answer was no—that which is trustworthy is not you, it is outside of you. All you have that you can trust is your reason, which will dictate that you should follow the social good. But if desire was bad, what was going to fuel my effort to obey reason? The unspoken answer was the same as the answer in childhood—fear. "Be responsible and be productive, *or else* . . ."

Such a fear-based mental construct increases reliance on external sources of control. These external controls become internalized as Self 1 concepts that judge both desire and behavior. As I lose touch with Self 2's natural instinct and am subject to the various cycles of Self 1 interference, there is a great price to pay in terms of human dignity, enjoyment, expression, and capacity for excellence.

Is There Natural, Self-Generating Ambition?—Maybe the most obvious word for the desire that motivates work is *ambition*. But this word has a somewhat negative connotation. Even my *Webster's* dictionary is ambiguous about its first meaning: "an eager and sometimes inordinate desire for something." My *American Heritage Dictionary* reflects the same ambiguity: "an eager or strong desire to achieve something, as fame or power." The famous funeral oration of Mark Antony comes to mind: "The noble Brutus/Hath told you Caesar was ambitious;/If it were so, it was a grievous fault;/And grievously hath Caesar answer'd it."

Grievous or not, *ambition* is a word that refers to a desire or aspiration of great strength. When it is called "blind ambition," it connotes a narrow focus that disregards the rights and legitimate concerns of others. It suggests also that the desire is so strong that it will not easily be deterred by the conflicting expectations or opinions of others or by priorities of less importance.

When I asked my son, in his first year of college, how he responded to the word, he replied, "Without it, you don't get off your ass!"

What I like about the word *ambition* is that it refers to a desire that is strong and comes from within. You don't think of teaching ambition. If you'll pardon the play on words, I like to think that we could call one's inherent desire *am*-bition, defined as a strong desire that comes from who I *am*.

To achieve an ambitious goal requires great effort that must come from great desire. When we set goals, whether as individuals, teams, or entire companies, we spend time and effort looking at the direction of our goals—i.e., what we want to achieve and *how* to achieve it—but not time examining whether there is sufficient desire to sustain the required effort to overcome the obstacles and carry through to fulfillment.

It has always been clear in sports that excellence requires desire. Talent and brains without the heart never win. So too, work requires ambition, and great work requires great ambition. Perhaps the reverse is even more true. Great ambition requires great work to be undertaken. If ambition is inherent in us in childhood, then what has happened to it? What have we done with it?

An Early Ambition to Excel—As a ten-year-old, I had a natural ambition to excel at touch football. It was one example of a desire that my environment (teachers, parents, and friends) supported. No conflict. My father would take me to Golden Gate Park in San Francisco to see football games during the days when Frankie Albert played for the Forty-niners. I was relatively small myself and admired this talented and fearless five-foot-ten quarterback. Watching him play football inspired my desire. I wanted to play like him, right then and there. Sometimes after the game, before the sun went down, I would be out on the street with the "gang," fading back to pass, left arm stretched out before me gauging the lead to give my receiver for a touchdown pass. Pure ambition. What I saw was what I wanted.

What is important to me about this is that no one had to tell me to try to pass like Frankie Albert, or teach me how. What I saw was a possibility and nothing told me I couldn't do it. There was no voice in my head that said, "He throws fifty yards and you only throw twenty." No put-down, no limitation, no inadequacy. Only, "I want to do it like that." And on occasion, my pass floated into the outstretched arms of my receiver for a touchdown with the same precision and the same results. The point is not that we can benefit from models, but that something within us can respond, can be inspired, and can then perform at ever-higher levels. It is that inherent capability I'm talking about. What matters is not how it works, but that it exists.

Our inherent ambition is the treasure of our treasures. Without it, no amount of talent and ability can produce value for the individual or society. Passion can be directed toward many different ends. One person might direct it toward fame in order to earn recognition and a sense of importance, another toward riches to ensure purchasing power, yet another toward political power. A mother and father might direct their passion toward their family. Many people may be ready to tell you how to direct your ambition, but they are not *you*. They can't know what you really want or what you should be listening for.

Listening for Felt Desire

Is work what I want or is it what I do when I have to stop doing what I want? Can I connect more strongly with the inherent ambition I felt as a child? I can at least decide to learn to "listen" for it.

An Experiment in Listening to the Voice of Self 2—Perhaps I could do an experiment, an exercise in listening directly to that felt desire. I could listen for what it has to say without preconception and just write what comes without censoring. I could do this experiment here and now and let the reader possibly eavesdrop. If I could learn to listen and write from this desire, it would be a step not yet taken in my own Inner Game.

I want to sing my song. I don't have time for anything else. Let this writing be worth my time.

These words are a surprise, yet they ring true. I feel more relaxed and my breathing is more noticeable. I can see that there is a choice to be made. I can listen to my thinking about what to write next, or I can listen to this feeling. I wonder if I dare let this feeling lead me to the words I am to write. Am I ready to acknowledge this feeling, granting it authenticity? It speaks as if it has something to say to me. Something different from what I might think of writing. What if I tried to connect with it? It feels as if I would have to relinquish a certain kind of control. Why do I hesitate? I don't know what "song" it will sing. Will it make sense? Will it be acceptable? To my reader, to myself? I feel more vulnerable than usual. I don't know what to expect. Yet I also feel excited by the possibility.

I will go with that feeling, go where it takes me, and listen to its song. Maybe that song will have something for me and for the reader. I don't know. I claim no mastery that can guarantee that these words will reach their mark. I will choose to stay true to this feeling, and follow where it takes me. I will write the words to the song that I hear there. I will continue to listen to this felt desire. I will try not to cheat it and make it into something it is not.

I am not a slave to anything. I do not work under pressure. I am someone who has something to reveal and who wants to reveal it. I am free and I only work freely.

Brave and confident words from this voice that seems so faint and gentle. It appears so much smaller than the voices demanding that I must get my work done. It is distinctly different from the voice of obligation and duty that counsels me to meet my responsibilities to others. That voice comes through loud and clear. The one I am now listening to has another tone and another message.

Be responsive to me. I am the feeling of you. I am original. I am where you can find joy in your minutes and hours.

I work for myself. I love what I do. I consider work one of the most wonderful opportunities of being alive. Work is my play. But it is play with a purpose. The purpose is mine. It is not your publishers'; it is not even your readers'. I am not just the author in you, the source of creative efforts. I am the you in you. I like expressing myself in many kinds of work.

What is also surprising me about this voice is that it is speaking in the present tense. It is not saying, "I want to be free." It is saying, "I am already free." I continue to listen to what it has to say to me.

I don't mind that there are deadlines. I don't mind that there are demands. They are the facts of the game you play. I don't mind the fact that when I play tennis, there is a winner and a loser, lines on the court, and a net to hit over—any more than I mind staying on the road when I am driving a car. Constraints in themselves don't bother me. They are like the banks of a river. I just like to flow, and I sense the ocean I am flowing toward. The riverbanks, the rocks, the changing slope of the riverbed, even the dams along the way, have nothing to do with the ocean I move toward. I flow because it is my nature to flow. I may not seem strong enough right now, but I do build up my own momentum. Drop by drop, I become quite a force. That's part of my nature, too.

Every time you listen to me, a drop is added to my river, and I grow. Drops become a rivulet. A rivulet meets with others and becomes a stream and soon a mighty river. This is how my desire grows. From a spark of interest to felt desire to a passion. With patience and some trust, I can become a river of passion.

This voice rings true to me. It is both familiar and unfamiliar at the same time. I pause to consider my choice. I am suddenly aware of the worried voice of my Self 1. "But what about your commitment to time lines? What about outlines and organization?"

I reply, "There is a time for that stuff, and this isn't it."

"But you are procrastinating. You are getting behind intentionally," the voice says accusingly.

I have been around the corporate workplace enough to know that I am not alone in this tendency to let the immediate take priority over the important. Isn't the feeling of being burdened and pressured by "all that's on my plate" a part of work for millions and millions of people? And behind all these pressures, there's the ever-present financial implication of not getting the job done on time.

Do I have a choice? Is feeling pressured an inevitable part of work? Must I simply put up with it and work on? The gist of everything I have written thus far is that I want something else. I desire to work freely. I desire to work in a mode that is quite different from being under pressure to get my work done. I know that I will never succeed in getting *all* the work done. The pile of unfinished tasks may decrease, but then it will build up again. Is it possible for me to get work done without feeling pressured? Is there another way? "Yes. You can work smarter and get more done in less time," says a rather superior-sounding voice in my head. Thank you, Mr. Consultant. I appreciate your advice. "You have to get better organized and then grind it out piece by piece," says another. Thank you, Mr. Taskmaster. Your advice is all too familiar. I don't discount that there is wisdom in what you say. But there is one part of me that doesn't completely buy into this conventional advice. It is the quiet desire that I sensed when the demands in my head were not so loud. Let me quiet down and listen again for the voice of my desire.

Demands from outside are there. Don't deny them. But see if you can't have them join our stream. We have been moving along pretty well in the past few minutes. We are moving in the right direction. You are enjoying this and some readers will benefit. Your deadlines will be met or perhaps they will not. The future is not entirely controllable. But let all your motivations join my river instead of trying it the other way around. Bring them along. I don't mind a little mud in my stream. I know how to use everything that enters me. My movement has a way of letting the mud settle to the bottom. In my river of freedom, the muddy waters of your pressured work will be clarified.

On the eve of your last day on earth, you will finally have no pressures. But it will be too late because you will also have no time. No time at all to know what freedom is. No time to know how a free man works or plays. No time to know me. I am really worth getting to know. Do it now. Join this river now. You can.

You have a choice about who you are working for, the outer demands or for me—the me that is you, the me that is already free. There is one

*other choice—to ignore that you have a choice. But then you will be the
force of that other river of demands—or rebellion against them, which is
just a tributary of the same muddy water.*

*You are liberated the moment you step across my boundary. You are free
to come and to go at your own choice. But come. Come simply because you
like it here. Come simply to be free. Understand the success in that.*

I have a client meeting in a half hour. There is not much time
to prepare. I feel vulnerable to the pressure of "not enough time."
I just want to keep things simple. I want to keep awake. It's important to me. Let's see what happens . . .

After the meeting, I return to my office and I take a short
STOP to reflect on the meeting. It had been as magical as when
playing my best tennis in the zone. The same economy of effort
for the results produced. I asked only a few questions and listened
fully to the client, who came up with ideas we both considered
original and practical. Nothing from the outside would have
seemed that remarkable. The meeting was devoid of any inner or
outer conflict. I thought that if all my meetings were like that, I
would not be worn down by the end of the day.

Later in the day, I receive a fax from the client. "For so long, I
have been feeling like a robot at work. Every day working mechanically and efficiently. Working, working, working! Our meeting woke up a part of me that has been so lifeless and has made for
a happier heart. Thanks . . ."

It's not uncommon to feel like a robot at work. Sometimes I
console myself with the idea that mechanization can feel like efficiency. But should I be consoled or disturbed by this mechanical
efficiency? I tell myself I am working efficiently if I get the job
done and in good time. Others will agree. Efficiency is measured
in terms of external results. But what about the other results? How
efficient was this work in terms of human results, in terms of the
impact of work on the worker?

This is the heart of the matter. As long as I define *work* as what
is accomplished externally, it is bound to be a one-dimensional re-

ward. But when I acknowledge that work makes a definite impact on the worker, it is a multidimensional game. Do you think you can count on your boss or supervisor to be interested in whether or not you are "working free," or whether you are becoming like a robot? Probably not. But doesn't that distinction make a huge difference to you? The robot in me can accomplish many results that bring compensation in terms of dollars and reputation. But without self-reflection and without awareness of my intrinsic nature as a human being, neither external results nor external compensation can measure the true value of my time.

Freedom from and Freedom For

I am an Irishman. And we Irish are famous for our rebelliousness. Whatever restricts the individual or assumes authority over it is fair game for rebellion. Yet the the freedom I seek cannot be won by merely pushing against the bars of the cage. The freedom I seek is not so much a "freedom *from*" as it is a "freedom *for.*" I remember the poignant example of a young bird that was placed in a cage with other birds. At first, it incessantly flew against the bars of the cage trying to get out. Its owners consoled it, pointing out the advantages of easy food and water, the nice swing, and the shiny mirror. Pretty soon the bird accepted its fate and stopped trying to get out. Then one day, a large bird alighted on the top of the cage and opened the cage door. Some of the other birds saw the open door and flew out. But our young bird didn't understand its meaning. He had forgotten how to fly.

The urge to work freely is not just about freedom from external constraints. It is not just about freedom from too many demands or not enough supplies. It is about gaining inward mobility as well as external mobility. It is about freedom to enjoy, to grow, and to be fulfilled. It is the freedom of the self that really is important—the one that since birth has wanted to enjoy and learn in everything it did. It is very easy to lose touch with our inherent selves in the face of external demands and especially while important institutions or people tell us that they are the most important. When we are surrounded by this message for years and from many different directions, it is difficult not to begin to believe it and to forget the self that has been largely forgotten by all but our closest friends. It's clear that the only way to remedy this situation is to begin to be our own close friends.

I give free rein to this long-quieted voice within me. It grows even more bold. I will not censor it. It speaks to me, and to you, if you care to eavesdrop.

Workers of the world, the chains that bind you are not held in place by a ruling class, a "superior" race, by society, the state, or a leader. They are held in place by none other than yourself. Those who seek to exploit are not themselves free, for they place no value in freedom. Who is it that really employs you and commands you to pick up your daily load? And who is it that you allow to pass judgment on the adequacy of your toil? Who have you empowered to dangle the carrot before you and threaten with disapproval? Who, when you wake each morning, sends you off to what you call your work?

Is there an "I want to" behind your "I have to," or have you been so long forgotten to yourself that "I want" exists only as an idea in your head? If you have disconnected from your soul's desire and are drowning in an ocean of "have to," then rise up and overthrow your master. Begin the journey toward emancipation. Work only in such a way that you are truly self-employed.

Ask yourself seriously, Do I have a master other than myself? Whose commands do I obey and what is the threat that stands behind these commands? The bonds to your internal master may be more difficult to break than any external chains. These are the less visible chains that bind your thought and your passion.

If one day you were to find the key to these chains in your own hands, would you open the gate and leave? Even if you were placed outside your prison by a benevolent hand and told you could leave, would you start looking for another safe prison? Saying "I want to be free" is easier than really wanting to be free.

So ask again, who are your jailers? Does the voice of your jailer seem to be that of your father, who perhaps was speaking in the voice of his father? Do you know where these commands had their start? Was it from a man-made god with rewards and punishments? Or was it a "god" of society whose public opinion you must embrace and whose approval you crave? These are formidable gods. Have you worshiped them for what they offer? Have you checked out for yourself what they actually deliver?

If you work, choose to do so without compromising yourself. Can you afford to do otherwise? Doesn't each moment of your life spent in servitude to meaningless demands take away a measure of your most precious resource, your time? Grant yourself hope. Ignite the flames of your determination.

Do not wait for society, your company, your boss, or your fellow workers. Do you have the time to wait? Be free yourself. Look not for permission or agreement, for you are alone. Look not for recognition outside of your own.

Work begins and ends with desire. All efforts to work free must eventually find their roots in one's own deepest urge. Only the voice that comes from that desire can steer you in the right direction. To work free, we must each learn to listen to its promptings. It is never too early or too late to begin such a journey.

About TEXERE

TEXERE seeks to become the most progressive and authoritative voice in business publishing by cultivating and enhancing ideas that will illuminate the global business landscape. Our name defines the spirit of our vision: TEXERE is the ancient Latin verb "to weave". In an increasingly global business community, we seek to create an intersection where authors and readers can share the best thinking and the latest ideas. We want to leverage the expertise and insights of leading thinkers by weaving them with TEXERE's capability to deliver them to the marketplace. To learn more and become a part of our community visit us at:

www.etexere.com

and

www.etexere.co.uk

About the Typeface

This book was set in 12/15 Bembo. This typeface was modelled on types cut by Francesco Griffo in Venice in 1495 for the book *De Aetnea* by Pietro Bembo, which dealt with his visit to Mount Etna. It is considered one of the first of the old style typefaces, that were used as staple text types in Europe for 200 years. Stanley Morison supervised the design of Bembo for the Monotype Corporation in 1929. It has well-proportioned letterforms, functional serifs, and lack of peculiarities. The italic is modelled on the handwriting of the Renaissance scribe Giovanni Tagliente.

About the Author

W. Timothy Gallwey attended Harvard Business School where he majored in English Literature and captained the tennis team. He is the author of the best-selling *Inner Game* series of books which he began writing in the 1970s. The *Inner Game* books set out a new methodology for the development of personal and professional excellence in a variety of fields. He is the founder of the Inner Game Corporation which applies the Inner Game principles to corporations looking for better ways to manage change. Through lectures, consulting and seminars, his focus has been directed at three main targets: helping all individuals within a company how to learn and think for themselves; helping managers learn how to coach; and helping leaders learn how to create "learning organizations". His long-term clients include AT&T, IBM, Arco, Anheuser Busch, Apple Computer and The Coca-Cola Company. He can be reached at The Inner Game Corporation, P.O. Box 875, Agoura Hills, CA 91376, USA or at http://www.theinnergame.com.

The *Inner Game* series of books:

The Inner Game of Golf
The Inner Game of Tennis
Inner Tennis: Playing the Game
Inner Skiing (with Robert Kriegel)
The Inner Game of Music (with Barry Green)